History at the Limit of World-History

ITALIAN ACADEMY LECTURES

Italian Academy Lectures

Umberto Eco, *Serendipities: Language and Lunacy*
Carlo Ginzburg, *No Island Is an Island: Four Glances at English Literature in a World Perspective*
Gianni Vattimo, *After Christianity*

History at the Limit of World-History

Ranajit Guha

COLUMBIA UNIVERSITY PRESS NEW YORK

COLUMBIA UNIVERSITY PRESS
Publishers Since 1893
New York Chichester, West Sussex

Library of Congress Cataloging-in-Publication Data

Guha, Ranajit
History at the limit of world-history / Ranajit Guha.
p. cm.—(Italian Academy lectures)
ISBN 0-231-12418-X (alk. paper)
1. World history. 2. Historiography. 3. History—Historiography. 4. History—Philosophy. I. Title. II. Series.

D20 .G756 2002
907′.2—dc21

2001047762

Columbia University Press books are printed on permanent and durable acid-free paper.
Printed in the United States of America

c 10 9 8 7 6 5 4 3 2 1

*To the memory of Ramram Basu
who introduced modern historiography in
Bangla, his native language, by a work published
two hundred years ago*

After such knowledge, what forgiveness? Think now
History has many cunning passages, contrived corridors
And issues, deceives with whispering ambitions,
Guides us by vanities.

—T. S. Eliot, *Gerontion*

Contents

Preface *ix*

1. Introduction 1
2. Historicality and the Prose of the World 7
3. The Prose of History, or The Invention of World-History 24
4. Experience, Wonder, and the Pathos of Historicality 48
5. Epilogue: The Poverty of Historiography—a Poet's Reproach 75

Appendix: Historicality in Literature by Rabindranath Tagore *95*

Notes *101*

Glossary *109*

Index *111*

Preface

This book has grown out of a series of lectures delivered at the Italian Academy for Advanced Studies in America at Columbia University in October–November 2000. The argument presented in those lectures has been amplified somewhat in an epilogue written for this publication. Translations from the Bangla original for the article in the appendix, as well as for all other passages included in the text, are mine.

Sanskrit words have been distinguished by diacritical marks throughout the text wherever required by grammar and convention. Words of Sanskrit origin written without any diacritical marking should be regarded as vernacularized.

I wish to thank David Freedberg, director of the Italian Academy, and his staff for their solicitude and generosity in providing me with excellent conditions for work at the academy during the term of my fellowship.

My thanks are due also to Andreas Huyssen, director of the Center for Comparative Literature and Society, and his colleagues Gayatri Chakravorty Spivak and Hamid Dabashi for the initiative they took to organize a two-day workshop around these lectures on behalf of the center.

I am particularly grateful to a number of friends who took time off in the middle of their busy academic schedules to read drafts of the manuscript in part or in full. They include Homi Bhabha, Akeel Bilgrami, Dipesh Chakrabarty, Partha Chatterjee, Nimai Chatterji, Nicholas Dirks, Amitav Ghosh, and Edward Said.

I owe a very special debt to Sankha Ghosh, the distinguished poet and critic. His advice has been of invaluable help to me in interpreting and translating Tagore for this work.

This book would not have been possible without the support and encouragement of Herbert Matis, director of the Institut für Wirtschafts- und Sozialgeschichte, Wirtschaftsuniversität Wien.

Jennifer Crewe, Anne McCoy, and Rita Bernhard of Columbia University Press have all, in their respective roles, helped in this publication. I should like to acknowledge here my very sincere appreciation of their kindness and many-sided cooperation in seeing this book through the press.

As always, working on this project has been an experience in companionship with Mechthild Guha who has been with me through all the agony and excitement it entailed from beginning to end.

Purkersdorf, Austria

History at the Limit of World-History

1 Introduction

The argument in this little book made up of three lectures and an epilogue continues in a direction taken some twenty years ago, but does so at a depth not sounded in my work until now. The critique of elitism in South Asian historiography was central to my concern at the time. In developing that critique I tried to show how the peculiarity, indeed the originality of Britain's paramountcy in the subcontinent as a dominance without hegemony, required the appropriation of the Indian past and its use for the construction of a colonial state. There was nothing in the structure or career of the Raj that was not fully involved in this statist enterprise. All of governance ranging from tax collection and land legislation through the establishment of a judicial system and a colonial army to the propagation of a colonialist culture by Western-style education and the promotion of English as the official language—every aspect of "England's Work in India" relied for its success on the reduction of Indian history to what James Mill was sagacious enough to claim as a "highly interesting portion of the British history." Which is why, I argued, it was up to the Indians themselves to try and recover their past by means of an Indian historiography of India.

All this, discussed at length in 1988–89 in an essay in *Subaltern Studies VI* and in my Deuskar Lectures, may perhaps be familiar by now to at least some of my readers from *Dominance Without Hege-*

mony (1997). However, I have come to realize that the plea for historiography's self-determination would be heeded more and understood better if the questions raised by it were addressed as they occurred progressively in the course of academic practice. For occur they must because of the intrinsically radical character of a project that calls on the colonized to recover their past appropriated by conquest and colonization. A call to expropriate the expropriators, it is radical precisely in the sense of going to the root of the matter and asking what may be involved in a historiography that is clearly an act of expropriation.

What is involved is not only the fact or force of conquest but its collusion with all aspects of colonialist knowledge. Everything that answered that description, whether as philology or political economy, travelogue or ethnography, or any other in a long list of arts and sciences, was party to such complicity, but none more so than philosophy overarching and comprehending them all. Philosophy owes this primacy to its power of abstraction, which enables it to assemble and arrange all the manifold activities and ideologies associated with colonialism under the rubric of Reason. One of the most influential exercises in such abstraction, and certainly one that is of direct relevance to what concerns us in these pages, is available to us in Hegel's writings on history. The phrase which succinctly sums up much of what he has to say on the subject, is *die Weltgeschichte*, rendered in English as "World-history" throughout this book with the hyphenation intended to emphasize its status as a concept rather than a description.

Hegel had inherited this term no doubt from the Enlightenment. But he elaborated on it and endowed it with a substantially new content until World-history came to be synonymous with "Reason in History." This is a view of history that allows all the concreteness to be drained out of the phenomena which constitute the world and its historicality. How such abstraction is brought about by the logic of *Aufhebung*, that is, "the act of superseding" whereby "denial and preservation, i.e., affirmation, are bound together," has been demonstrated by Marx in some of his commentaries on Hegelian texts. He shows, for instance, that, in *Elements of the Philosophy of Right*,

> *civil law* superseded equals *morality*, morality superseded equals the *family*, the family superseded equals *civil society*, civil society superseded equals the *state*, the state superseded equals *world history*.

The outcome of this serial *Aufhebung* is to displace these entities from "their actual existence" and transform each of them into a philosophical concept so that, says Marx,

> my true religious existence is my existence in the *philosophy of religion*; my true political existence is my existence in the *philosophy of law*; my true natural existence, my existence in the *philosophy of nature*; my true artistic existence, existence in the *philosophy of art*; my true *human* existence, my *existence in philosophy*. Likewise the true existence of religion, the state, nature, art, is the *philosophy* of religion, of nature, of the state and of art.[1]

By the same token, historicality as the true historical existence of man in the world is converted by the act of superseding into philosophy of history and the concreteness of the human past made to yield to the concept of World-history. Which is why that concept and the uses to which it has been put in Hegel's philosophy of history will engage us in the argument developed in these pages.

Aufhebung amounts to the "transcending of a conceptual entity," as Marx points out in his reading of a parallel series from the *Encyclopaedia* where each term transcends the one that has gone before. "Thus, private property *as a concept* is transcended in the *concept* of morality," and so forth, until the last term, *absolute knowledge*, emerges hierarchically as the highest in which all the others are dissolved and affirmed at the same time.[2] In much the same way, the order of supersession in the aforementioned series taken from the *Philosophy of Right* culminates in the transcendence of World-history by the concept of God or *Geist*, as it is made clear not only in that text but in Hegel's *Lectures on the Philosophy of World History* as well.

Transcendence entails, in this last instance, a claim to superior morality in favor of World-history. The latter, constructed transcendentally into a providential design, "can be seen as a theodicy, a justification of the ways of God," according to Hegel himself.[3] And "what we call God" is, to put it in his own words, "goodness, not just as a general idea but also as an effective force." Thus World-history, "the plan of providence," acquires an aura of moral sanctity by definition, while the state, a key link in the chain of supersessions and the agency that promotes such a plan as the "concrete manifestation" of "the ethical whole," comes to "constitute ethical life" itself.[4]

It is in this way that World-history managed to reach the high moral ground climbing on the back of philosophy. The latter, for its part, has proved itself truly to be a child of the Age of Imperialism. Going by Plutarch's story about that meeting between Diogenes and Alexander in Corinth, there was a time when philosophers were eager to keep their distance from world conquerors.[5] Not so in the post-Columbian era when it would be possible for one of its most distinguished thinkers to write

> world history moves on a higher plane than that to which morality properly belongs. . . . The deeds of the great men who are the individuals of world history . . . appear justified not only in their inner significance . . . but also in a secular sense. But from this latter point of view, no representations should be made against world-historical deeds and those who perform them by moral circles to which such individuals do not belong.[6]

Our critique, which stands at the limit of World-history, has no compunction whatsoever in ignoring this advice. From the point of view of those left out of World-history this advice amounts to condoning precisely such "world-historical deeds"—the rape of continents, the destruction of cultures, the poisoning of the environment—as helped "the great men who [were] the individuals of world history" to build empires and trap their subject populations in what the pseudo-historical language of imperialism could describe as Prehistory.

The critique is happy, therefore, to join issue with World-history, deny it the moral license for which Hegel pleads in the extract cited above, and pay no heed to his warning about "the much discussed and misunderstood dichotomy between morality and politics."[7] On the contrary, it is our intention here precisely to confront the philosophically certified "higher morality" of World-history with its politics by asking some difficult questions about the morality of colonizers claiming to be the authorized historians of lands and peoples they have themselves put under a colonial yoke. We do so not only to set the political record of colonial rule straight in such general terms as have any bearing on our discussion. What concerns us more is the representation of the colonial past held in thrall by a narrowly defined politics of statism.

It is the inadequacy of historiography that has alerted us to this thralldom. Seen from the perspective of the colonized, that inadequacy is nothing other than a measure of the dominance exercised by a mode of colonialist knowledge. Sponsored and propagated by the Raj, it has had the effect of replacing the indigenous narratologies of precolonial times by ones that are typically modern and Western. The statism so firmly entrenched in South Asian historiography is an outcome of this narratological revolution which has, by its very success, prevented us as historians from apprehending it as a problem. Incorporated in World-history, we owe our understanding of the Indian past, our craft, and our profession as academics to this very revolution. We work within the paradigm it has constructed for us and are therefore far too close and committed to it to realize the need for challenge and change. No wonder that our critique has to look elsewhere, over the fence so to say, to neighboring fields of knowledge for inspiration, and finds it in literature, which differs significantly from historiography in dealing with historicality.

As discussed in the epilogue, historicality has not been assimilated to statist concerns in literary representation according to Rabindranath Tagore, the greatest South Asian writer of our age. The past, he believes, renews itself creatively in literature, unlike in academic historiography with its insistence on keeping its narratives tied strictly to public affairs. The power of what he has to say in this respect lies not only in its independence. It obviously owes nothing to the guild that has reduced the study of the past to a blinkered colonialist knowledge. What is more important is the wisdom that informs his observations. It is wisdom born of the experience of living dangerously close to the limit of language as one must to be a truly creative writer. For it is the latter's vocation to exhaust language and push it to the brink. Which is why Tagore had learned to recognize a limit when he saw one, and the limit of World-history could hardly escape so keen a poet's eye. However, his reproach about the poverty of historiography is not only a comment on the failure of the genre but also a call to historians for a creative engagement with the past as a story of man's being in the everyday world. It is, in short, a call for historicality to be rescued from its containment in World-history. Our critique is our response to that call.

2 Historicality and the Prose of the World

The concept of limit—the Renaissance idea of "people without history"—Hegel on India: "No state, no history"—the instance of Ramram Basu—history and prose in Western thinking—the distinction between prose and poetry according to Vico and Condillac—statehood and prose as conditions of eligibility for World-history status—the twofold character of prose in Hegel's philosophy of history—the prose of the world: how it disrupted the primal unity of the age of poetry—intersubjectivity and the struggle for mutual recognition between self-consciousnesses—the everyday and the notion of temporal particularity—opening up the prospect of a historiography adequate to historicality.

To start with, let us consider the name given to this book. What, one may ask, does the word *limit* have to do in the title flanked by a referent seemingly so illimitable as *World-history*? The answer is that it is there precisely to provoke a question like this and bring out in relief the obviousness taken for granted, so that it may be questioned in its own turn. If *limit*, as defined by Aristotle, is "the first thing outside which there is nothing to be found and the first thing inside which everything is to be found,"[1] its function in the title may be understood as a signal of our attempt to explore the space beyond World-history. In other words, we shall try and think World-history in terms of what is unthinkable within its boundaries. In this attempt to probe the limit of historical thinking we follow Wittgenstein. To draw a limit to thought, he says, "we should have to find both sides of the limit thinkable (i.e. we should have to be able to think what cannot be thought)."[2] Accordingly in our move towards a thinking of historicality as what cannot be thought, we shall set out from that side of World-history "inside which everything is to be found," taking the concept of "people without history" for our point of departure.

We owe this concept, among other things, to the navigational errors and adventures which led to the conquest of America. It is well known that apart from violence and plunder legitimized simply by hoisting a flag in the name of a king or queen, this was also the occasion for a comprehensive exercise in discrimination. Thanks to it, Renaissance Europe learned to identify itself by the otherness of a multitude of races, religions, languages, and cultures. Names and categories were invented to enable the knowledge systems of the Old World to cope with the exigencies of the New. One such invention that was to find a place for itself fairly soon in the expanding lexicon of alterities is the concept "people without history."

Presupposed in that phrase was a view of history which, according to Walter Mignolo, had already been assimilated to the historiography of the period giving currency to "the idea that people without writing were people without history and that people without history were inferior human beings."[3] For the conquistadors, the people excluded thus from history and pushed to its margins were the conquered themselves—the Amerindians. It would take the idea another three hundred years to reach South Asia and put the subcontinental Indians beyond the pale of history as well. Here again the strategy was the same as in the previous instance—that is, a joint operation of wars and words, modified only to the extent that the wars were to be British and the words German.

Three centuries was a lot of time of course. Meanwhile, guns and gunboats had grown in size. Equally, if not more significantly, the hands and minds that deployed them were those the West had put at the helm of each of its emergent nation-states. Philosophy was attuned to this development at an early stage, as already apparent from some of Kant's political essays. But it was left to Hegel, caught up as he was in the ebb and flow of the European revolutions of his time, to lay the foundations of a comprehensive philosophy of history with the question of the state at its core. A people or a nation lacked history, he argued, not because it knew no writing but because lacking as it did in statehood it had nothing to write about. He dismissed the Amerindians as "obviously unintelligent" and spoke of them as "unenlightened children" distinguished only by "inferiority in all respects." The states in South America were "still in the process of formation," according to him, while even in North America "the universal purpose of the state [was] not yet firmly established," the influx of Europeans notwithstanding.[4] In 1830, when these words were written, the continent as a whole was, presumably, still without history just as Columbus had found it.

India was a different matter altogether, culturally speaking. Hegel, unlike James Mill, his English contemporary, had nothing but admiration for its intellectual achievements. But these did not qualify it for statehood in his view. The promise of some development in that direction was "incipient" in the earlier phase of "social distinctions" among its people, but came to nothing as these "petrified into natural determinations—i.e. the caste system." Which is why India has no history, he says. This is a comment that punctuates his observations like a refrain. Thus,

> It is obvious to anyone with even a rudimentary knowledge of the treasures of Indian literature that this country, so rich in spiritual achievements of a truly profound quality, *has no history*.

And again,

> India not only has ancient religious books and splendid works of poetry, but also ancient books of law. . . .; nevertheless, it *still does not have a history*.

These extracts taken from the Second Draft of the *Lectures on the Philosophy of World History* indicate how the rules for admission to

World-history had changed between the adventures of Hernando Cortes and those of Robert Clive.[5] The bar was raised, so to say, by a few notches. Writing was still regarded as a necessary condition, but not sufficient. A people had to have statehood to qualify fully. Since writing to be historical needed the state to write about, it was subsumed in the latter. The Renaissance formula, "No writing, no history," so popular with the conquistadors, was updated by 1830—the year of the Second Draft—to read, "No state, no history." The revision followed inexorably from the logic of historical developments in the West. The formative energies and expansionist drives of its new nations would henceforth be invested in the state as the locomotive of that most modern and dynamic of inventions called World-history.

Yet the nexus in which history, historiography, state, and writing were so intimately joined, was not free from anomaly. For unknown to Hegel, the limit he imposed on history at the mark of statehood had already proved to be a line drawn in the sand. He is clearly in error in insisting, as he does in 1830, that India, with all its intellectual and spiritual resources, "has no history"; and I quote him again to underline his use of the present tense: "It still does not have a history." The evidence is against this pronouncement. A work on Indian history, the first of its kind written by a Bengali in his own language, but done in conformity with the Western model of historical writing, was published in Srirampur (anglicized often as Serampore) in the neighborhood of Calcutta in 1801, and it was not the only one of its genre to appear in print during the next three decades.

What does that make of World-history and India's exclusion from it? For an answer let us start with a quick look at that first specimen. It was commissioned by William Carey of Fort William College set up by the English East India Company in 1800 at its eastern headquarters in order to train its European employees in the use of the major languages of the country they were learning to govern.[6] Carey, a Christian missionary, who headed the Bangla department of the College, had "no books or helps to assist" in teaching and relied on the indigenous scholars who worked under him to produce the manuals he so badly needed. Ramram Basu, a junior pandit, was asked "to compose a history of one of their kings."[7] Basu obliged by writing *Raja Pratapaditya Caritra* in Bangla, his mother tongue. It was hailed at once as "an authentic history of the government of Bengal from the beginning of the reign of Achber to the end of that of Johangeer."[8] Since then, succeeding generations of political and literary historians—Nikhilnath Ray and Jadunath Sarkar amongst the former and Sushil Kumar De and Sisir Kumar Das amongst the latter—have examined the text critically for its use of evidence as well as for its narrative mode. It has not escaped their notice that the author allowed his story to lapse occasionally into myth and fantasy; but they all agree that this flaw—almost unavoidable under the circumstances—has done little to undermine the overall authenticity of the work as an exercise in modern, rationalist historiography.

This is an assessment with which Basu himself would have readily agreed. For he takes care to distinguish his work clearly from the tradition of Persian chronicles that had been in vogue since the beginning of Mughal rule and flourished under the patronage of the court and regional elites. There is a little bit (*kincit*) written about Pratapaditya in the Persian language, he says somewhat vaguely without referring to any texts by name. But whatever may be there by way of such accounts is, he maintains, fragmentary and incomplete (*sanga panga rupe samudayik nahi*). It is nothing that can satisfy the curiosity of those who want "to know the story of that prince from beginning to end (*anupurbik*)."[9] There is something patently modernist about this insistence on continuity and completeness—all that sets the proper historical narrative apart from the premodern annal and chronicle.[10] One understands, therefore, why William Carey was so proud to announce the forthcoming publication of Basu's manuscript as it was on its way to the printers in the summer of 1801:

> I *got* Ram Boshu [Ramram Basu] to compose a *history* of one of their kings, the first *prose* book ever written in the Bengali language; which we are . . . printing.[11]

Here, according to Carey, was a double first for an Indian language—the very first instance of its historiography and that of its prose—both achieved under the aegis of colonialism, for it was the missionary acting for the Company's government who "got" the native to write the book that he did. However, the claim is somewhat exaggerated. He was right to speak of Basu's work as the first Western-style historical narrative in Bangla, but not as "the first prose book ever written in the Bengali language." Yet the importance of this error is hard to overestimate. It illustrates the connection between history and prose that had come to be taken for granted in the West by that time. Indeed, we have in Carey's description not only a record of what he found so exciting about the work commissioned by him. More important, it allows us to see how by the end of the Age of Enlightenment two of the most powerful movements of contemporary Europe—one in politics and the other in thought, that is, the drive for overseas expansion and the passion for history—happened to intersect in an apparently small detail of South Asian life. Long before the first modernist historian of Bengal was to sit down to write his narrative in prose, the latter had already been assimilated to a global process of historicization.

For, since Columbus, Europe had been obsessively engaged in voyages of self-discovery requiring it to try and match the coordinates of intercontinental space by those of universal time—geography by history. This exercise relied on a new mathesis of comparison. Climates and habitats, customs and polities, belief systems and phonic systems of the most diverse kinds were all collected and displayed side by side on epistemic spreadsheets to be measured and calculated for their worth on a civilizational scale standardized in the West. Since civilization stood for progress in time, the scale itself was identified with history enriching its concept with discriminations and differentials it had not known before.

Language was one of those spreadsheets of knowledge at which European science and imagination were incessantly at work for four hundred years between the Discovery of America and the Scramble for Africa. But even before the formation of comparative linguistics as a special field of studies a delicate but clear distinction between poetry and prose had emerged from this exercise. Poetry was assigned priority on the temporal scale. Correspondingly, the status it gained on the scale of values was that of the originary and the primordial. Neither the sanctity associated with the former nor the mystic of the latter applied to prose. Subsequent and younger, its time was regarded as that of the everyday world and its values as mundane and modern.

Although such a distinction was generally agreed on, not all thinkers approached it in the same way. Indeed, some of the most important amongst them testified in effect to its power and range by using it for historical scenarios that had little in common. Early in the eighteenth century Giambattista Vico had already identified the first language of man—the foundational language of laws and religions—as poetic. For him the origin of poetry was independent of human design. It was, he believed, "a proof of Providence."[12] By contrast, Condillac was to take a more secular view of the same phenomenon. In *An Essay on the Origin of the Human Language* (1746) he would trace the beginnings of poetry to a remote past when languages were not rich enough in structure and vocabulary to serve the entire range of human needs. Consequently people "adopted all sorts of figures and metaphors" and had recourse to mimicry and pleonasm to make up for the deficit. Thus it was the "sterility of languages" and a primitive "mode of speaking by action" that made communication "originally poetical" by force of necessity. "But in proportion as languages became more copious," he writes, "the mode of speaking by action was abolished by degrees, the voice admitted of less variety of tone, the relish for figures and metaphors . . . insensibly diminished, and their style began to resemble our prose." It was the philosopher Pherecydes of Scyros who, "disdaining to be fettered by the rules of poetry," we are told, "first . . . ventured to write in prose."[13]

Condillac was convinced that his story of progress from poetry to prose was a genuinely "historical account."[14] Jacques Derrida contests this claim. All this talk about "the history of language" as "the human spirit," he protests, is nothing but "history as a narrative retracing a prescribed progress, a natural progress . . . only the development of a natural order."[15] Even if there is a role for "men of genius" in this account, that does not make progress any the less natural for the younger philosopher who cites Condillac's own words: "When I say *men of genius*, I do not exclude nature whose favorite disciples they are."[16] If this is an attempt to trap Condillac in self-contradiction, I am not sure it succeeds. For, "men of genius" do not cease to be human just because they happen to be the "favorite disciples" of nature, nor, by the same token, does a "natural" progress or development, mediated by them, lose its entitlement to historicity.

Indeed, by bringing man and nature together into his explanation of the origins of language Condillac not only maintained his consistency but helped to historicize a phenomenon which had been shrouded in mystery until then. He belonged to an age that was seized by an insatiable curiosity about the newly discovered languages but baffled at the same time by their multiplicity, diversity, and complexity. It was almost inevitable that his attempt to reach these at their source, like that of many of his contemporaries, should occasionally get mired in speculation. He was modest enough to acknowledge the difficulty. "Some perhaps will look upon this whole history as a romance," he remarked toward the end of the *Essay*, "but they cannot at least deny its probability."[17] He was not, of course, the only thinker of the period to enlist probability in support of history. For the beginning of poetry and prose, generally of language, was still hidden in a past beyond evidence, relics, and memories. In that darkness one could only grope for some primordial clump of roots. Amongst those who believed they had found it, Vico spoke of it as a gift of God, and Condillac as a gift of nature. The latter, to my mind, stands for a considerable advance in historical thinking.

But the scene shifts again with Hegel turning to the question early in the next century. For him, the priority of poetry over prose had little to do with the economy of language and an initial state of poverty overcome eventually by expansion into prose. Poetry and prose figure in his thinking as terms of development in a rather different sort of history—that of Spirit (*Geist*) itself. The latter is, according to him, an indivisible totality which comes to know itself and achieve self-consciousness through a process of self-division, self-opposition, and, finally, reintegration. This is a movement of becoming—"a *conscious*, self-*mediating* process—Spirit emptied out in Time,"[18] and is, as he put it, "the labour which it accomplishes as actual History."[19]

In this history, poetry was the first to emerge from Spirit's labor. But it was prior to prose logically as well. At this stage, says Hegel,

> It is the original presentation of the truth, a knowing which does not yet separate the universal from its living existence in the individual, which does not yet oppose law to appearance, end to means, and then relate them together again by abstract reasoning, but which grasps the one only in and through the other.[20]

It is the function of prose to disrupt this unity by the force of individuation. Under its impact all that is whole and integral splinters into the utmost relativity. History, both as a writing about the past and as the past it writes about, feeds on this prose. But even then it is not a sufficient condition for the production of history. That condition is provided by the state, according to Hegel. "It is the state which first supplies a content," he says, "which not only lends itself to the prose of history but actually helps to produce it."[21] How to explain, then, that thirty years before this formulation India, described by him as historyless and stateless, had already succeeded in producing its first history and first work of prose by an indigenous author? Excluded from World-history by definition, Ramram Basu and his writing seem to have sneaked across the border somehow.

This is not a puzzle solved readily by reference to any precolonial tradition of annals and chronicles, if only because these, too, go back to a time before state formation, hence before history, according to the Hegelian chronology. Nor can Basu's historiography be traced to an educated acquaintance with English historical literature. He had a smattering of English—*alpasvalpa ingreji-jnan*—according to Brajendranath Bandyopadhyay.[22] But that did not stretch beyond the requirements of rudimentary conversation with his mentors among the Christian missionaries, as one of them observed, somewhat patronizingly, at the time: "He is a very sensible man; speaks English pretty well, though he cannot read it."[23]

The achievement of this humble employee of Fort William College—an assistant pandit with a salary of forty rupees per month—is that it takes us to the limit of World-history, although it does so from the inside. To recall what Wittgenstein says, one must approach a limit from both sides. Starting off from the inside, we have come upon a phenomenon that enables us precisely to do so. With nothing to show for itself except an unself-conscious audacity that defies the Hegelian scheme of things, it opens up a vista of historicality beyond World-history. What to make of this transgression, so naive and yet so radical in its implications? Does it mean that philosophical thinking of the kind under discussion has overextended the sign "World" by compounding it with history? One wonders if it has not indeed exceeded its semantic competence to endow universality on what is no more than a regional experience of writing history in a condition of statehood. To put it another way, a particular manner of thinking about the past has perhaps been inflated into a genre—*vyakti* into *jāti*. The work of Ramram Basu, mere gravel that stops World-history in its globalizing track, incites us to break out of this generic containment and join historicality on the other side of the border.

In order to do so, it will help, first, to inquire what kind of containment it is and how it works. It is written large over Hegel's texts, paradoxically, by the liberal use made of two of the most inclusive phrases one can think of—namely, prose of the world and prose of history. World and history: taken together, they add up to a space big enough, one would have thought, to house all of historicality. But that did not happen: several continents and their populations were still left out of history. To understand why, let us consider how in this usage prose relates to world and history. Linked by a semblance of uniformity, prose here stands both for a condition of language and a condition of being. The frequent and surprisingly fluid traffic between the two is characteristic of much of Hegel's writings on history and accounts, to an extent, for some of their turns and twists.

The twofold prose belongs to a hierarchy of stages in Spirit's progress towards self-realization in history. To start, in ascending order, with the prose of the world, it signals the end of the primordial unity celebrated by poetry since the beginning of time. In that undifferentiated universe nature had been conspicuously lacking in mediation between "life in general" and the living individual. The division of genus into species and of species into individuals made no difference in this regard. Unable to break away from their originary bonding with the earth and its environment, all such "moments of simple determinateness" would be absorbed in "the process of Becoming merely as a contingent movement." For, as Hegel reminds us, "organic Nature has no history." By contrast, "Spirit is time," and the prose of the world heralds the advent of consciousness—"the middle term between universal Spirit and its individuality or sense-consciousness." The latter mediated in its own turn by the "structured shapes" that consciousness assumes as "a self-systematizing whole of the life of the Spirit," realizes "its objective existence as world-history."[24]

We are now at the inaugural moment of history. Consciousness has triumphed in the unity of the universal and the individual. The uncomplicated integrity of the age of poetry has dissolved to open up the world so that Spirit can actualize itself in a myriad relativities. It marks the triumph of individuality, which had never been more free. A discrete and isolated drive that had nothing to do so far other than to reproduce itself cyclically in nature, it would now combine that function so essential to species-being with the particularity of a self-consciousness related to other self-consciousnesses. For particularity, we know from the logic of reflective judgment, connects the immediate individual predicatively with something else. Thus to say "This plant is medicinal" is to regard the subject, plant, "as standing in connection with something else (the sickness which it cures) by means of its predicate (its medicinality)." Or, to cite yet another of Hegel's examples on this point, "Man as *this* man, is not this single man alone; he stands beside other men and becomes one in the crowd."[25] By the same token, to speak of any individual as self-conscious is to relate him at once with other self-conscious individuals endowing history thus with an inexhaustible concreteness. This is what Jean Hyppolite has called intersubjectivity.[26] In the *Phenomenology* it is the epiphenomena of *Geist* itself as "the unity of the different independent self-consciousnesses which, in their opposition, enjoy perfect freedom and independence: 'I' that is 'We' and 'We' that is 'I.' "[27] But it is precisely such exchanges between "I" and "We" that make the history involved in all this much more than an episode in Spirit's career. The interplay of these self-consciousnesses constitutes the human condition itself. As Hegel puts it, "Self-consciousness exists in and for itself when, and by the fact that, it so exists for another; that is, it exists only in being acknowledged."[28] This amounts, of course, to a "double movement" in which two self-consciousnesses are related in such a way that "each sees the *other* do the same as it does; each does itself what it demands of the other, and therefore also does what it does only in so far as the other does the same." Consequently, each serves as the middle term for the other, so that through this process "they *recognize* themselves as *mutually recognizing* one another."[29]

It is this process of recognition that takes us to the very core of the prose of the world. We have seen that world present itself in the aspect of individuality to allow self-consciousnesses to emerge in freedom. However, particularity as the second aspect of the development makes sure that the self-consciousnesses are, for all their independence, related to other things by means of predication. If the interconnections so formed stand for prose, their worldhood may be said to be affirmed in mutuality. For it is in the dynamics of mutual recognition that the prose of the world finally comes to its own, fulfilling the promise of individuation and particularization. This makes for a most interesting world identified usually by two of its great philosophical landmarks—the unhappy consciousness and the dialectics of master and slave. But there are some passages, less known because buried in the massive tome of the *Aesthetics*, where the concreteness of that world is presented in a broad outline with Hegel saying: "Here is revealed the whole breadth of prose in human existence."

What he refers to is an intricate web of relativities formed by self-conscious individuals "recognizing themselves as mutually recognizing one another." Mutual recognition requires that the individual, "in order to preserve his individuality," must lend himself as a means to others for use to satisfy their interests and reduce others to mere means as well to satisfy his own interests at the same time. Consequently, he can never be "an entirety in himself" in the eyes of the others who come to know him and deal with him only in terms of "the nearest isolated interest which they take in his actions, wishes, and opinions." Furthermore, the individual subject is also defined by his dependence on such externalities as laws, customs, social and political institutions, and so forth, "which he just finds confronting him, and . . . must bow to . . . whether he has them as his own inner being or not." In short, it is precisely by trying to make his individuality secure through mutual recognition that man alienates himself. Anticipating latter-day thinking about that predicament by about a hundred years, Hegel writes:

> The individual as he appears in this world of prose and everyday is not active out of the entirety of his own self and his resources, and he is intelligible not from himself, but from something else.[30]

But alienation is only one of the features of "this field of relative phenomena," the other being fragmentation. The participation of an individual even in the great actions and events of his community's life can help little to lift his effort above the level of a mere trifle. This applies not only to the common man but in some ways, if not quite to the same extent, also to "those who stand at the head of affairs." For everything is caught up in the particularity of "circumstances, conditions, obstacles, and relative matters." There is nothing that is whole. All is dissolved in a mass of details. "Occupations and activities are sundered and split into infinitely many parts, so that to individuals only a particle of the whole can accrue." Summing up his survey of the concreteness of a highly complex and relativized world where individuals connect with one another as alienated and fragmented beings involved in a struggle for mutual recognition, Hegel observes:

> This is the prose of the world, as it appears to the consciousness both of the individual himself and of others:—a world of finitude and mutability, of entanglement in the relative, of the pressure of necessity from which the individual is in no position to

> withdraw. For every isolated living thing remains caught in the contradiction of being itself in its own eyes this shut-in unit and yet of being nevertheless dependent on something else, and the struggle to resolve this contradiction does not get beyond an attempt and the continuation of this eternal war.[31]

Clearly this tangled and volatile prose relies for its dynamics on the individual interacting with others to constitute a world. And that, of course, is nothing other than the familiar everyday world. Which goes to explain why "prose" and "everyday" and their derivatives shadow each other so closely in Hegel's writings. A certain outlook is described as a "mode of *everyday* consciousness in our *prosaic* life"; some German authors are taken to task for representing "*daily life*" in rather "*prosaic*" terms; Protestantism with its "sure footing in the *prose* of life" is credited to have inspired Dutch genre painting to seek its subjects in "*daily* life;" and so forth.[32] And as already mentioned, it is in a "world of *prose* and *everyday*" that the individual is called on to join the game for two to play. Everyday stands thus for the temporal dimension of the prose of the world.

This is an essential dimension. It determines the concreteness of the I-We transactions which give that prose its content. For it is in the everyday that individuals encounter one another in the process of mutual recognition. It is there that they have or do not have time for others. In short, it is the everyday that provides the prose of the world with a basic framework on which to display the fabric of intersubjective relationships as the phenomena that constitute it. Consequently we do not have to stretch the idea too far to think of everyday as the general form of the temporality that informs the prose of the world.

Expressed in this form everyday appears initially and obviously as the present. However, this is a present distinguished by a forward lurch even as it makes its debut. For what drives a self-consciousness to seek another with which to negotiate recognition is desire. According to the *Phenomenology of Spirit*, "Self-consciousness is *Desire* in general."[33] As such, it stands clearly apart from need. Unlike the latter, it is not directed towards any sensuous object in particular with which to satisfy its appetite. "What it desires, although it does not know this explicitly, is itself," says Hyppolite; "it desires its own desire. And that is why it will be able to attain itself through finding another desire, another self-consciousness. . . . Desire seeks itself in the other; man desires recognition from man."[34] But this proves to be an endless pursuit. For any recognition whatsoever is superseded at once to give rise to desire for another, constituting an interminable series of successions. Desire, as Jacques Lacan has observed, is thus "caught in the rails" of metonymy "eternally stretching forth towards the *desire for something else*."[35] If self-consciousness is the movement of desire, it is inexorably forward-moving. That is how, as a participant in the everyday struggle for recognition, it propels what is present in the prose of the world necessarily towards the future.

But this is not all that is there to the temporality of the prose of the world. Its everyday present, ever on its way to the future, is laden with the past as well. For each individual brings along with him a past as part of the equipment he must have for his encounter with an other. Correspondingly, the particularity, thanks to which he has been caught up in the mesh of interconnecting subjectivities in the first place, turns into a *temporal particularity* predicated on a specific past. This temporal particularity mediates the everyday being-together-in-the-world of all who have time for one another. The past figures in this mediation as a set of reciprocities with the subject arriving at the scene as someone with a history. The other he is about to meet has a history as well. Thus history stands, in each case, for the experience of what he has been so far as a particular being in body and soul, and what in his past has not only induced him to enter the game of recognition but also determined the other with whom he will be involved in that game and how the latter will proceed. Each will bring his own history to the process of recognition as an essential condition of its mutuality.

However they will do so in terms of an answering movement that complements for each the knowledge of his own past by an interpretation of the other's he does not know yet. What he knows, or thinks he knows, is only his own history. Yet recognition demands that he should know the past of the other as well. Understanding gets to work, therefore, to make sense of the latter by providing the preconceptions and presuppositions an individual needs as foreknowledge or intuition that runs ahead of itself about what he is connecting with. The other he connects with reciprocates in similar terms. In this way, each in his predisposition acquires a grasp of the other's past as material that is already available for historicization. The prose of the world in which human beings make one another intelligible in the course of their everyday struggle for mutual recognition becomes imbued thus with historicality.

If the writing of history were to ground itself in such historicality, it would have a subject-matter as comprehensive as the human condition itself. The world would open up with all of its pasts ready to serve for its narratives. No continent, no culture, no rank or condition of social being would be considered too small or too simple for its prose. On the contrary, we would be ushered into a complex universe "of finitude and mutability, of entanglement in the relative, of the pressure of necessity from which the individual is in no position to withdraw."[36] As one can see from this description, it would be the world of the prose of the world itself. And what stories it would have to tell!

It may not be too idle to speculate that Hegel himself was excited, however momentarily, at the prospect of a historical discourse embracing "the whole breadth of prose in human existence," that is, the prospect of a historiography fully adequate to historicality. After all, he had seen the light of a dawn awakening and enlarging the world of his early academic days in Tübingen. Perhaps a glint of that vision still lingered in his aging eyes when he wrote to remind the historian that he had "no right to expunge these prosaic characteristics in his material" and that, to all circumstances, characters and events confronting him, "he must give free play in their external contingency, dependence on other things and uncounselled arbitrariness." For it is in the historical situation, he says, that "the play of chance" reveals itself as "the breach between what is inherently substantive and the relativity of single events and occurrences as well as of the particular characters in their own passions, intentions, and fates." Thus history as "this prose" of the world has, in his view, "far more things that are extraordinary and eccentric than those miracles of poetry."[37] He goes on, therefore, to warn the historian against the temptations of poetry.

> If the historian carries his subjective inquiries [he writes] so far as to probe the absolute reasons for what happens and even Divine providence, before which all accidents vanish and where a higher necessity is unveiled, nevertheless, in respect of events as they appear in reality, he may not allow himself the privilege of poetry.[38]

Ironically, however, the philosopher was to succumb to that temptation himself. Not long after he had written this cautionary advice into his lectures on aesthetics, he would exercise "the privilege of poetry" in his lectures on the philosophy of World-history. He would do so in the name of a prose of history devised strictly according to divine providence. Not only that "events as they appear in reality" would be hitched to "a higher necessity" cutting out contingency and arbitrariness. But entire continents and peoples would be cut out of history as well. Except for a region of relatively developed statehood and designated, with some exaggeration, as World-history, the greater part of the prose of the world with all its historicality would be left to stagnate in "prehistory." How and why this happened will be the subject of our discussion in what follows.

3 The Prose of History, or The Invention of World-History

Advent of the prose of history—its role in developing a historiography to display Spirit's progress as Reason in History or World-history—dynamism of the process of actualization—the idea of historical "stages" in Condorcet and Hegel—the shift in Hegel's thinking toward a notion of history as providential design—centrality of statehood in the criteria of eligibility for World-history—the principle of exclusion and Eurocentric bias underlying the Hegelian schema—the category of Prehistory and its implications—the politics of displacement in the philosophy of World-history as seen from the other side of the limit.

The prose of history comes after the prose of the world as a staging post on Spirit's road to self-consciousness. Here, no less than in the instance of primal differentiation between poetry and its successor prose, it is the younger that is more developed, more progressive. For, in Hegel's evolutionary model, the subsequent is distinguished by a higher value. "In the case of spiritual phenomena," he writes, "higher forms are produced through the transformation of earlier and less advanced ones."[1] Nothing testifies better to this order of precedence and importance for Hegel than the emergence of the prose of history out of the prose of the world, a new prose out of the old. In the *Aesthetics* he shows how the latter constitutes a field of particularities, conflicts, and contingencies with the Spirit still not free from its entanglement with nature. It will have to assert its freedom and through freedom achieve self-consciousness by objectifying itself in the concreteness of the world. World-history will draw for its content precisely on this process of Spirit's self-objectification, and it will be for the prose of history to conceptualize and write it. And since Spirit is reason, World-history and its representation in historiography stand for reason in history—a phrase made famous by the subtitle of his *Lectures on the Philosophy of World History*. However, years before that publication he had already constructed a nexus relating World-history to reason and Spirit thus in *Elements of the Philosophy of Right* (1821):

> Since spirit in and for itself is *reason*, and since the being-for-itself of reason in spirit is knowledge, world history is the necessary development, from the *concept* of the freedom of spirit alone, of the *moments* of reason and hence of spirit's self-consciousness and freedom. It is the exposition and the *actualization of the universal spirit*.[2]

Actualization is of strategic importance in this formulation. For, it is thanks to actualization that "the spirit attains its most concrete reality" in what Hegel calls the "theatre, province, and sphere of [its] realization [as] the history of the world."[3] But actualization presupposes potentiality, that is, what is still implicit and holds itself back until finally achieved as a goal attained or an object grasped. It might be tempting, therefore, to think the potential in the image of a germ, except that it could lead one to believe Spirit's actualization in history as being somehow similar to what happened in nature. But the analogy does not work, and Hegel cautions us by pointing out that "in nature, [Spirit] actualizes itself only as the other of itself, as dormant spirit," whereas in the state—and by implication in history—Spirit "which is present in the world . . . *consciously* realizes itself therein."[4] This is a significant distinction, which corresponds, in Hegelian ontology as developed in the *Encyclopaedia*, to that between being as "unreflected immediacy" and existence as the "immediate unity of being and reflection [,] hence appearance." The latter makes itself explicit as an externality which is its "energizing," as Hegel calls it.[5] He chooses, therefore, to characterize potentiality as an impulse ("just as the Aristotelian *dynamics* is also *potentia*," he reminds us)—the "inherent impulse of spiritual life to break through the shell of natural and sensory existence, of all that is alien to it, and to arrive at the light of consciousness, i.e. at its own nature."[6]

Actualization is thus the process by which Spirit overcomes the natural determinations of its being to assert its freedom and take to the path of its realization in self-consciousness. It is a dynamic process that suggests a great deal of movement on the road to reason. For what is at issue here is "the aim of world history," as Hegel puts it, to assimilate itself to Spirit's career, so "that the spirit should attain knowledge of its own true nature, that it should objectivise this knowledge and transform it into a real world, and give itself an objective existence."[7] The truly historicist character of this aim, "itself a product of the spirit," shows up in a passage bristling with temporal indices. Thus:

> This *process* [of actualization], in which [Spirit] mediates itself with itself by its own unaided efforts, has various distinct moments; it is full of *movement* and *change*, and is determined in different ways at different times. It consists essentially of a series of separate *stages*, and world *history* is the expression of the divine *process* which is a graduated *progression* in which the spirit comes to know and realise itself and its own truth. Its various *stages* are *stages* in the self-recognition of the spirit; and the essence of the spirit, its supreme imperative, is that it should recognise, know, and realise itself for what it is. It accomplishes this end in the *history* of the world; it produces itself in a series of determinate forms, and these forms are the nations of world *history*. Each of them represents a particular *stage* of *development*, so that they correspond to *epochs* in the *history* of the world.[8]

Process, movement, change, stages, progression, development, epochs: words which seem to bear out the dictum that "the utterance of the actual is the actual itself."[9] Witness to Spirit's labor at actualization in World-history, they are marks left by that project on the sands of time. They speak of its drive and direction, its transformative energies, its imprimatur on the designation of ages and periods. But it is the phrase "stages" that stands out of this welter most clearly to define Spirit's involvement in history and measure its extent. For a stage is a resting place that punctuates the line of an ongoing movement. If Spirit were on its journey in the world, a stage would indicate how far it had traveled, how much farther it had to go, where it had stopped and for how long. But a stage is also a platform used for display as in a theater, and World-history is, for Hegel, "the theatre in which we are about to witness [*Geist*'s] operations."[10] In undertaking thus to put the latter up for show on the stage of World-history, the philosopher assumes the role of impresario or producer—the wise man who, as an accomplice of Spirit itself, already knows the plot. Or he may be acting as the *sūtradhāra*, the controller of the story line, who, in a Sanskrit drama, could also be the *vidūṣaka*, i.e., the jester. If the stage is meant to display Spirit's performance in the world not merely for entertainment but also for the evaluation of what it has achieved, the prologue can make a difference depending on who delivers it. I leave it to my audience and readers to identify the figure they first see on the stage when the curtain goes up. Is that the philosopher of history or history's fool?

For our part, let us get on with the show taking "stage" in the first of these two senses for cue. We do so because it refers Hegel's thinking back to its roots in the Enlightenment and points at the same time to an orientation that is all its own. Throughout the eighteenth century the European mind had been occupied with speculations about progress as it made its way through the world along a path called history. And with the world expanding in space under the impact of conquests and discoveries and in time by contact with the older civilizations, the road became long and arduous enough to require an occasional stop between one lap and the next. The metaphor of progress as a journey in stages was an attempt made by the philosophical language of the time to grasp this movement. It was a legacy Hegel had acquired in direct line of descent, but what he did with it would not have amused the forefathers.

Take Condorcet, the last of the *philosophes* to write on the history of progress. His *Sketch for a Historical Picture of the Progress of the Human Mind*, published in 1795, sums up a great deal of what the most eminent intellectuals of the century, Voltaire and Turgot amongst them, had to say on this subject.[11] It is a magisterial survey of progress as a journey in ten stages and the remarkable thing about it is that it is firmly set in the world. There is nothing about it, nothing that connects its stages or makes up their content as history, which is not strictly secular. Universal history, as constructed by the Enlightenment, might have differed between some versions and others in scope and interpretation. But they all had man at the center. Which is not what one could claim for Hegel's construction of World-history.

Hegel scholars have noticed a remarkable shift in his thinking between an earlier youthful phase and another that was more mature dating from the Jena days. Nothing so clear-cut as a lurch from left to right, it was nonetheless conspicuous for the caution that had displaced the radical enthusiasm of his Tübingen period. The revolutionary wave of the 1790s had peaked and passed and with it was gone what Charles Taylor calls "the man-centred conception of regeneration" characteristic of Hegel's ideas in his early theological manuscripts. He would now proceed to match the "notion of *Geist* as a subject greater than man" to "a notion of historical process which could not be explained in terms of conscious human purposes, but rather by the greater purposes of *Geist*." Henceforth "the subject of history in Hegel's thought" would no longer be man but *Geist*.[12] All this is copiously documented in the later writings and especially in the *Lectures on the Philosophy of World History*, as the following extracts show:

> World history is nothing more than the plan of providence. The world is governed by God; and world history is the content of his government and the execution of his plan. (p. 67)

> The overall content of world history is rational, and indeed has to be rational; a divine will rules supreme and is strong enough to determine the overall content. (p. 30)

> That world history is governed by an ultimate design, that it is a rational process—whose rationality is . . . a divine and absolute reason—this is a proposition whose truth we must assume; its proof lies in the study of world history itself, which is the image and enactment of reason. (p. 28)

Since World-history is a providential plan, Hegel insists that it is not and cannot be subject to arbitrariness, chance, or anything else that may imply contingency. In the *Logic* he acknowledges the part played by contingency in nature and "in the world of Mind" as well. However, it is up to science and philosophy, he says, to realize that for them "the problem . . . consists in eliciting the necessity concealed under the semblance of contingency."[13] Accordingly, in the *Lectures on World History* he proceeds "to eliminate the contingent" by taking his stand on what he considers "the religious truth that the world is not a prey to chance and external contingent causes, but is governed by providence."[14] The outcome of the exercise, as noted above, was to found history on *Geist*'s design. The very embodiment of reason, it was destined fully and faultlessly to realize itself by matching its end to its concept and the concept to the process of its actualization.

The problem with this design to cast history in cement, albeit in the name of God, is that it is hardly amenable to the practice of historiography. Immune from contingency it is obviously not subject to those mediations which alone can transform the potential into the actual. In other words, it is frozen in a condition outside time and history. The discourse for such a design may, arguably, be a kind of hard-eyed objectivist description with no room for interpretation in it. Whether it is possible to conceive or write such a discourse is itself an intriguing question. But leaving that aside, it may be difficult in any case to write the story of Spirit's journey through the world if its freedom is not free enough to slip into uncertainty or its itinerary is indeed so secure as never to be upset by accident.

We know, of course, that in his lectures on World-history Hegel has sought to cover himself preemptively against the charge of inflexibility. He has done so, first, by allowing passion a certain amount of play in its encounter with reason and, secondly, by the proviso that the execution of *Geist*'s plan may run into difficulty, or contradiction as he calls it, in particular instances of its working at the national level. But these allowances, made in an empiricist gesture, apply only to the local and the incidental without affecting the cosmic design. Fortuitous exceptions, they highlight the fundamentally inexorable aspect of the latter. There is no room for irony in this history. It may put up with the occasional titter and tickle at the margin, but no laughter to mock the providential discipline on guard at the center. All of which must make the story of the past very dull reading indeed. But can such a history be written at all?

The question seems to have occurred to Hegel as well. That is why at a critical turn in the argument—between remarks on the principles governing Spirit's development and those on the stages of its progress—he pauses briefly to reflect on historiography:

> [Development] contains not just the purely formal aspect of development itself, but involves the realization of an end whose content is determinate. And we have made it clear from the outset what this end is: it is the spirit in its essential nature, i.e. as the concept of freedom. This is the fundamental object, so that the guiding principle of development endows the development itself with meaning and significance; thus, in Roman history, Rome is the object which guides our consideration of the events, and conversely, the events have their source in this object alone, so that their entire significance and import are derived from it.[15]

This, to me, is a statement about method according to which the writing of history requires a selection of material (or evidence, as historians call it) that is relevant to the theme, topic, or problem written about. Any decision I take in this regard will serve as a "guiding principle" to determine the choice of evidence—generically speaking, "events"—and endow them with significance as they go into the making of my narrative. Handled with care this method might work. With care—one cannot emphasize that enough—so as not to use the terms of the principle concerned as blinkers and deny evidence the freedom to interact with hypothesis and plot correcting the flaws in one and infelicities in the other.

But even if I were to adopt this method for my history, I would still hesitate to follow Hegel's example in naming it. For the name should be true to the nature of the exercise so that no one is misled about its scope. Since the scope is itself strictly circumscribed by the governing principle which nominates the theme and selects the content for my narrative, I would have to designate it in accordance with these determinations, just as "Roman history" is named after Rome, the "principle" that in Hegel's view thematized the history so called and furnished it with all the relevant "events." Working by this analogy, as the philosopher expects his readers to do, it would be hard for them to justify "World History" as title or description of *his* narrative.

It is a narrative about the development of Spirit, which, we have been told, is "a form of progress."[16] The end or aim of progress is Spirit's realization of itself "in its essential nature, i.e. as the concept of freedom," and this is what, in Hegel's opinion, "endows the development itself with meaning and significance." In other words, the story, which has this development as its "object," relies on "the guiding principle" to select its *matériel* from the world where Spirit realizes itself as freedom in the course of its progress. The world is witness thus to the progressive self-realization of Spirit and provides evidence for its narrative. But that does not make the latter World-history any more than an account of Marco Polo's travels in China makes his travelogue a history of China. The subject of Hegel's philosophy of history is *Geist* and not the world.

Yet this hypostasis has its uses. As an Indian, I recognize in this an idealist device similar to what the ancient school of Vedānta called *adhyāsa*. Translated into English usually as "superimposition," it functions as a basic concept in the theory of illusion (*māyāvāda*), and means, according to Śaṅkara, the ninth-century philosopher (788–820 A.D.), "the apparent presentation of the attributes of one thing in another thing."[17] This is conventionally illustrated in the texts by the analogy of seashell (*śukti*) mistaken for silver (*rajata*) with its metallic sheen superimposed on the other's translucence. In much the same way, the Spirit overdetermined by the world generates a space for ambiguities of all kinds, the most relevant of which is, for us, the confounding of *Geist*'s development with historical progress. It will be assumed henceforth that these movements, which are supposed to be concurrent, almost coincidental, follow the same path and are grasped best by the understanding with the help of a common set of signposts. Installed to indicate the stages of a journey, these are used to promote an easy exchange of attributes between the fellow-travelers making the historicization of Spirit hard to distinguish from the spiritualization of history.

Hegel leaves us in no doubt about the importance he attaches to these stages, which, he says, "supply us with the divisions we shall observe in our survey of world history and which will help us to organise our discussion of it."[18] This is somewhat of an understatement. For it is obvious that their function in the text, as it unfolds, is much more basic than that of sectional markers or editorial devices. They describe the conversion of the prose of the world into the prose of history in terms of Spirit's progress towards freedom and self-consciousness. This involves, first, the choice of a set of basic "principles" as the means of historicization; secondly, some general considerations about natural and historical change; and, thirdly, the formulation of conditions required for what should or should not count as history. We shall discuss these in turn.

1. Let us start with Hegel's dictum that "world history as a whole is the expression of the spirit in time" and recall that he modifies it at once by adding, "But in one respect, the nations of history, which are spiritual forms, are also natural entities. Accordingly, the various patterns they assume appear to coexist indifferently in space, i.e. to exist perennially."[19] He then goes on to enumerate and describe these "patterns" as "three main principles"—the Asian principle (including the Chinese and the Indian), "the first to appear in history"; the Middle Eastern or Islamic principle of monotheism "coupled with unrestrained arbitrariness"; and "the Christian, Western European . . . the highest principle of all." These constitute, for him, a "universal series . . . existing perennially," and encountered as "a se-

quence of successive stages."[20] In other words, it is the function of the latter to reify timeless entities and designs for history by overlaying them in a regional schema. No wonder, then, that such historicization has imbued Hegel's construct of World-history with all the usual ambiguities of superimposition confounding seashell and silver, or, as in the present case, the regional and the universal.

2. The concept of stages is used next as a guide to the dynamics of history. This calls for a critical distinction between changes in nature and those in "the spiritual world," which is often the name Hegel uses for history. "Changes in the natural world," he says, "no matter how great their variety, exhibit only an eternally recurring cycle; for in nature there is nothing new under the sun."[21] It is not that things do not change in nature; they do, but only as individuals to be reproduced in the species. It is a world trapped in its own particularity: here, "the life which arises from death is itself only another instance of particular life." The result is a cyclicity thanks to which "the survival of the species consists purely in a uniform repetition of one and the same mode of existence."[22] By contrast, anything that is new emerges "only in those changes which take place in the spiritual sphere."[23] It does so, because "in the world of the spirit, each change is a form of progress." Here, unlike in nature with its reproductive cycles always churning out the same, "higher forms are produced through the transformation of earlier and less advanced ones." Which is "why spiritual phenomena occur within the medium of time"—that is, history.[24]

However, the distinction between linearity and cyclicity concerns not only the shape or form of change but its character as well. As Hegel points out, "The development of natural organisms takes place in an immediate, unopposed, and unhindered fashion, for nothing can intrude between the concept and its realization, between the inherently determined nature of the germ and the actual existence which corresponds to it." This is a relatively "peaceful process" that allows growth to retain its identity and remain "self-contained in its expression." But there is nothing so smooth about the path taken by Spirit. The process of its actualization is mediated by consciousness and will which "are themselves immersed at first in their immediate natural life." Consequently they tend "to follow their natural determinations" pulling away from the direction of Spirit's urge "to fulfil its own concept."

All this makes progress "a hard and obstinate struggle" for Spirit, which "divided against itself . . . has to overcome itself as a truly hostile obstacle to the realisation of its end."[25] History, considered thus, appears as a turbulent scene of perpetual restlessness and uneven development. Its linearity, not to be mistaken for simplicity, is charged with tension and conflict. Its movement, always at transverse to the self-containment of nature, is characterized by an inexhaustible dynamism ready for investment in that open and unlimited prospect we have come to recognize as the prose of the world.

3. The division between the stage of Spirit's immersion in nature and that of its emergence in the fullness of history is a preliminary, though necessary, step for our understanding of World-history. It provides us with what at one point Hegel calls "the a priori structure of history to which empirical reality must correspond."[26] Much of the *Lectures on the Philosophy of World History* is an exercise in fitting structure to reality and demonstrates what kind of world the author had in mind—and what kind of history.

It is in the course of this exercise that the stages are put to their most effective use not simply as narrative breaks but as integral to the argument itself. They have a dual function in this regard. They punctuate a lateral movement insofar as Spirit is on a journey in time. However, it is evolutionary as well, ascending from lower to higher forms. In that vertical construct the stages stand for a corresponding order of values rising from base to apex in a pyramid of civilizations. We have already come across these values as immanent in a number of "principles" constituting a universal series for Hegel. Now they will be woven, strand by strand, into time's warp to make up the fabric of history. As a classic of the idealist view the design is known quite well and requires no comment except to highlight an aspect left out of consideration by most writers on the subject.

They have discussed it at length for its metaphysical and political implications, but seem not have noticed a lacuna in the pattern. What is presented there as the subject of World-history turns out, on closer look, to be no more than a region claiming to speak for the world as a whole. Consequently the history that goes with it proves to be highly reductive in scope—a short story with epical pretensions. The story belies the global and almost aeonic gesture of its title by leaving large chunks of historicality out of the plot. This is made abundantly clear by the strategies of exclusion used for this purpose.

Hegel had no intention to hide the exclusive character of his schema. In the First Draft of the lectures on World-history—a term used throughout the "Introduction" synonymously with "universal world history" and "philosophical history of the world"—he defines its scope thus at the very outset:

> Nations whose consciousness is obscure, or the obscure history of such nations, are . . . *not the object* of the philosophical history of the world, whose end is to attain knowledge of the Idea in history—the spirits of those nations which [have] become conscious of their inherent principle, and have become aware of what they are and what their actions signify, are its *object*.[27]

Those who are lucky enough to qualify as the object of World-history are thus categorically distinguished from those who are not. Henceforth the excluded will be settled in a space called Prehistory with World-history reserved solely for the chosen nations. The line separating Prehistory and World-history—the upper case used to indicate their status as strictly demarcated areas of history—is drawn at consciousness. For *Geist*, the World Spirit, uses national spirits [*Völkergeister*] to actualize itself in the historical process, which is "the movement of its own activity in gaining absolute knowledge of itself and thereby freeing its consciousness from the form of natural immediacy and so coming to itself." In other words, self-consciousness assumes national "configurations" [*Gestaltungen*] in the course of its liberation from "natural immediacy."[28] These configurations—the Oriental, the Greek, the Roman, and the Germanic—four "world-historical realms" Hegel calls them (or three when the second and third are conflated on some occasions) are then allocated to the partitioned zones to make up a diptych of philosophical history.

Which configuration will be allocated where depends, first, on the degree of its lack of "immersion in nature," and, secondly, on the extent of its affirmation of freedom. Both of these conditions are satisfied by the emergence of the state, which is regarded as a true measure of the maturity of a national spirit's self-consciousness. For, according to this view, it is by constituting a state that a people or nation (*Volk*) frees itself from its thralldom in "natural immediacy." With all the incipient and weak formations left out as inadequate it is only a fully developed statehood that qualifies nations for their place in World-history.

Three out of the four realms pass the adequacy test. The only one that fails is the Oriental. It does so because, as the very first of the configurations to emerge in time, it has not moved beyond the moment of "absolute beginning of every state's history" at which "*spirituality* is still *substantial and natural*."[29] However, this observation, which dates from the *Philosophy of Right*, is modified subsequently in the *Lectures on World History* where Hegel identifies the condition as "that so-called unity of the spirit with nature which we encounter in the Oriental World."[30] Whether it is a case of arrested development that could occur anywhere or just a typically Eastern phenomenon, this indicates, in any case, that Spirit is "still immersed in nature and not yet self-sufficient; it is therefore not yet free, and has not undergone the process by which freedom comes into being." Compared to the other realms where *All* are free as in the Germanic, or at least *Some* are as in the Greek and the Roman, only *One* is free in the patriarchal world of the Orient.[31] The latter, born before all the others—speaking in terms of stages—is trapped, paradoxically, in a condition of spiritual infancy, while Greece and Rome have pushed ahead respectively to youth and "manhood." However, Hegel, fond as he is of organic analogies, does not extend this one to the Germanic instance, which he describes as "the old age of the spirit." Old age, he says, is followed by death in the case of human beings, whereas Spirit cannot die, "so that the comparison is no longer applicable."[32] Rather ingenious, one may think. But let that pass. For it makes no difference to the Oriental's place in the sequence of stages. Lagging behind the rest of the pack on the road to self-consciousness or stuck at the bottom of freedom's tower—no matter whether the image of progress is lateral or vertical—the Orient is condemned to remain where it was at the very beginning—that is, condemned to stay frozen in Prehistory.

But is there no redeeming feature or factor at all? Is there nothing in, for instance, the great literatures, philosophies, and arts of India and China to entitle them to a niche in World-history? Hegel's answer is an emphatic no. He addresses this question again and again, and deals with it vigorously and at length on each occasion. In his writings of the later years he would return to the scene on the slightest pretext and often by the longest detour to deliver yet another blast, as if he felt he had not said enough already and the matter was far from settled. He did not deny that creativity and morality could be "encountered in every region, under all constitutions, and in all political circumstances" and that India and China were indeed remarkable for their achievements in this respect. Yet when it came to dealing with the favorable opinion expressed by some scholars about Indian or Chinese philosophy as compared with Eleatic, Pythagorean, and Spinozistic metaphysics, he reacted strongly to join issue with them. He dismissed their views as abstractions lacking in "determinate content." This implied, according to him, "that those distinctions which ar[o]se out of the degree of self-consciousness which freedom ha[d] attained [were] unimportant or inessential" for the advocates of a less restrictive view of history.[33]

What he means by "determinate content" and "distinctions" in this context is clarified further in his own evaluation of Chinese morality and Indian philosophy. The former, known in Europe through the writings of Confucius, has received, he notes, "the highest praise and the most flattering tributes to its merits even from those who are familiar with Christian morality," while the latter has been admired for the sublimity of its argument against "all sensual things."[34] However, he is not impressed. In his opinion,

> These two nations are lacking—indeed completely lacking—in the essential self-consciousness of the concept of freedom. The Chinese look on their moral rules as if they were laws of nature, positive external commandments, coercive rights and duties, or

> rules of mutual courtesy. Freedom, through which the substantial determinations of reason can alone be translated into ethical attitudes, is absent. . . . And in the Indian doctrine of renunciation of sensuality, desires, and all earthly interests, positive ethical freedom is not the goal and end, but rather the extinction of consciousness and the suspension of spiritual and even physical life.[35]

His critique of the Indian epics does not stray much from this line of attack. He is not insensitive to their charm, he admits with a touch of condescension, but finds that in the subcontinent, as elsewhere in the East, this particular kind of poetry does not allow the individual "to work his way through to that independence of personal character and its aims (with the collisions that these involve) which the genuine development of dramatic poetry imperatively demands."[36] The human element "remains repressed" here. In the Rāmāyaṇa and the Mahābhārata man figures as a sort of apanage of the gods—either as an incarnation of one of them or as a mere accessory or simply as an entity assimilated to godhood by ascetic practices. In Greek poetry, by contrast, gods and men enjoy "freedom of independent individuality."[37] Hegel's verdict on Indian literature is indeed as negative as it is Eurocentric: "The substantive foundations of the whole thing are of such a kind," he writes, "that our Western outlook can neither be really at home there nor sympathize with it because we cannot resolve to abandon the higher demands of freedom and ethical life."[38]

Whether this has to do with philosophy or epic poetry, India just does not make the grade. For even in these fields of high achievement it does not know freedom. However, this freedom must not be mistaken for any particular will free to pursue its own ends. It stands for the freedom of each individual citizen to try to identify himself consciously with the general will—that is, the state. As Hegel puts it: "Freedom is nothing more than a knowledge and affirmation of such universal and substantial objects as law and justice, and the production of a reality which corresponds to them—i.e. the state."[39] Which leads us to the heart of the matter: the peoples and nations of the Oriental realm are excluded from World-history because, according to the philosophy that has constructed it, they have not matured fully into statehood.

The centrality of the state in Hegel's system is a well-known fact of Western philosophy, and so are the debates it has inspired. He is firmly of the opinion that the process of Spirit's actualization in the world culminates in the state. All the salient aspects of that development are reiterated in various combinations tirelessly in his statements on the subject. In one he would speak of its implications for history, freedom, and will, thus: "The state is the spiritual Idea externalised in the human will and its freedom. All historical change is therefore essentially dependent upon the state, and the successive moments of the Idea appear within it as distinct constitutional principles."[40] Elsewhere, taking history together with freedom, the state is said to be "the more specific object of world history in general, in which freedom attains its objectivity and enjoys the fruits of this objectivity."[41] Reason and existence, too, are served best by the state. "Only in the state does man have a rational existence," he says. "Man owes his entire existence to the state, and has his being within it alone. Whatever worth and spiritual reality he possesses are his solely by virtue of the state." Truth is assimilated as well: "For the truth is the unity of the universal and the subjective will, and the universal is present within the state, in its laws and in its universal and rational properties."[42] And to cover everything as comprehensively as possible there is that coping pronouncement in the *Philosophy of Right* according to which "the state consists in the march of God in the world."[43]

All that is, of course, metaphysics, which, however, has not stopped Hegel's critics from questioning its politics. His own method invited such questioning. As a child of his times he had his thinking colored inevitably by the events and sentiments of that epoch. "No philosophy can transcend its own age," says Jean Hyppolite, "or jump over Rhodes, as Hegel puts it." And Marx was one amongst a number of contemporaries and near contemporaries to identify "an essential tendency of Hegelian thought, which is to legitimate existing reality by conceiving it philosophically."[44] Whether that amounted to a bias in favor of Prussianism or made his theory of the state into an instrument for "the preparation of fascism and imperialism," as suggested by Ernst Cassirer, may be open to argument.[45] But it is beyond doubt that the continuing debate on this question for the greater part of two centuries is itself evidence of what so radical a statist doctrine like Hegel's can do to perpetuate the fear of strong, centralized states and totalitarianism. However, the implications of such statism for historiography and generally for our understanding of history have not been a part of that liberal concern. For the latter it is only the doctrinal threat to Western European democracy that is a political issue, but not the exclusion of other peoples and continents from history. Prehistory is just prepolitical according to this view, whereas regarded from the standpoint of the excluded it is nothing other than political.

The line which divides World-history and Prehistory is itself an obvious clue to that politics. Obvious, because it is a line clearly drawn on the map. The three realms out of the four—the last three stages—are all European ranging successively, between antiquity and modernity, from the Greek through the Roman to the Germanic. Hegel's use of the word "Germanic" (*germanisch*) is very broad indeed. It includes not only what he calls "Germany proper" (*das eigentliche Deutschland*) with its Franks and Normans, and the peoples of England and Scandinavia—generally, the Teutons—but also the "Romanic" peoples of France, Italy, Spain, and Portugal with the Lombards and Burgundians, the Visigoths and Ostrogoths, and moving somewhat to the east, even the Magyars and the Slavs thrown in for effect.[46] That adds up to about all of Western and Central Europe, as we know it.

Hegel identifies himself spontaneously with the region when he speaks in the name of a collective "we" to express his disapproval of something Oriental—as, of the Indian epics, in the instance cited above. Some of that self-identification might have induced him to bend his own rules of adequacy in order to admit the three European realms to World-history. Its gates are firmly shut, for instance, against India which does not qualify because its society is an unfree patriarchal structure, but the slave societies of ancient Greece and Rome do and so does medieval and early modern Europe with its tolerance of slavery and its considerable dependence on servile labor. China and India are "out" because in these polities only One, that is, the despot, is free, while Greece and Rome are "in" with the stipulation about fully developed freedom modified to accommodate the fact that Some, though by no means All, are free there. The Germanic realm may have benefited from some special consideration in this respect as well. Here All are supposed to be free, for it is a "Christian World," and, says Hegel, "In the Christian age, the divine spirit has come into the world and taken up its abode in the individual, who is now completely free and endowed with substantial freedom."[47] This is a very tall claim to make and one that is altogether without foundation in the facts of European history, even if it were drastically foreshortened to date the beginning of "the Christian age" from the fall of the Roman Empire. What about freedom in the principalities and kingdoms ruled by despots and oligarchs throughout the region in that period with only One free in some cases and no more than Some in most of the others? What about the "freedom of All" under the absolute monarchies, all very Christian, which had ruled over large parts of Europe for three hundred years until Hegel's time?

The discrimination that allows the conditions of eligibility for World-history to be suspended or modified in favor of Europe and strictly enforced against the rest of the world follows from Hegel's theory of state. Considered in the light of his evolutionary idea of progress it is a Darwinist theory somewhat ahead of its time, but one with no pretension at all to scientific neutrality. On the contrary, the triumph of the strong over the weak is not only regarded as necessary but justified according to some primordial and presumably superior sense of right and wrong. It is "the *right of heroes* to establish states," he says in the *Philosophy of Right*. It matters little whether the exercise is benevolent or violent or even evil in an ordinary sense of the word, for what is involved is the Idea objectified and actualized in the deeds of the hero acting as its agent.[48] In the *Aesthetics* he refers to Hercules as one such hero—"not exactly a moral hero," he grants, judging by his lust on the Thespian night or his brutality at the Augean stables, but a hero nonetheless who, like other "Greeks of his kind," appear in a pre-legal era, or become themselves the founders of states, "so that right and order, law and morals, proceed from them."[49]

What holds for such heroes holds for "civilized nations" as well and *"entitles [them] to regard and treat as barbarians other nations* which are less advanced than they are in the substantial moments of the state (as with pastoralists in relation to hunters, agriculturists in relation to both of these), *in the consciousness that the rights of these other nations are not equal to theirs and that their independence is merely formal.*"[50] The argument is extended thus in a number of ways. In the first place, it is not concerned with the individual hero but with "civilized nations." Secondly, the site has moved from myth to history with the "civilized" representing higher modes of production and states corresponding to them as compared to those of the "barbarians." Thirdly, right, conceptualized no longer in absolute terms by reference to the Idea or *Geist*, has been secularized in this instance as what actually obtains among nations and relativized according to degrees of difference between economies, states, and civilizations. And, finally, "in the wars and conflicts which arise in these circumstances," the so-called civilized nations are entitled to treat the barbarians as peoples whose rights are not equal to theirs and whose independence is "merely formal," hence not worth respecting.

Thinly veiled in philosophical language there is something in this formulation that all students of colonialism will recognize straightaway as the notorious right of conquest. It is the sort of right that encouraged the first architects of the British empire in the East to dismiss questions about the East India Company's legal entitlement to rulership in the subcontinent as "mere formalities," and boast, as one of them did before the House of Commons, "There was no power in India but the power of the sword, and that power was the British sword, and no other."[51] The man who carried that sword for the Company, Robert Clive, was obviously not far from Hegel's mind when he cited him as an example of the morality of conquest. Clive, regarded from the standpoint of the conquered as less of a hero than a crook who had luck on his side, represents in the *Philosophy of Right* "the true valour of civilized nations" and "their readiness for sacrifice in the service of the state."[52] The fact that he worked throughout his career only for a merchant company and never for the state at a time when the two were not on the best of terms is a detail which seems to have been overlooked in statist haste. For the main thing is to uphold the primacy of the state, even by anticipation if need be, and do so by glorifying the imperial projects of European powers as a moral and spiritual achievement.

To stop such achievement from being trivialized as the triumph of a superior force in "any ordinary war between nations," Hegel rolls out a wide literary canvas to display the violence of territorial aggrandizement as a "higher undertaking . . . grounded in a higher necessity." That, he says in a passage remarkable for its candor,

> arises above all in the Iliad where the Greeks take the field against the Asiatics and thereby fight the first epic battles . . . that led to the wars which constitute in Greek history a turning-point in world-history. In a similar way the Cid fights against the Moors; in Tasso and Ariosto the Christians fight against the Saracens, in Camoens the Portuguese against the Indians. And so in almost all the great epics we see peoples different in morals, religion, speech, in short in mind and surroundings, arrayed against one other; and *we are made completely at peace by the world-historically justified victory of the higher principle over the lower*. . . . In this sense, the Epics of the past describe the triumph of the West over the East.[53]

Hegel could have called that the triumph of World-history over Prehistory as well. The conceptual demarcation between these two terms in his writings on the philosophy of history coincides neatly with one that is geographical. As such it enables us to grasp the politics of its metaphysical phrasing by translating the so-called "victory of the higher principle over the lower" as that of "civilized" Europe over the "barbarians" of already colonized and yet to be colonized Asia, Africa, and Latin America. We who hail from those parts are posited by this geopolitics clearly at the lower end of the arch that spans millennia between the age of Homer and that of Columbus—the age of imperialism.

Hegel's inclination "to legitimate existing reality by conceiving it philosophically" has been the object of a great deal of comment in the West, but mostly for its regional implications, as we have noticed. Western scholars have only been concerned to justify or refute the notion that his radical statism contains elements hostile to the liberal-democratic state system of the West itself. It is therefore up to those excluded from World-history by that statism to try and understand what such segregation implies for historicality on the other side of the line of demarcation. This, I know, is easier said than done. It demands a lot of rethinking and involves the pain of unlearning what one has learned to take for granted in historiography. Which is perhaps why this is a task best left to an entirely new generation of intellectuals with eyes less tired than ours and minds less committed to shibboleths. They will see and think better. All we can do is to take some steps towards identifying and enunciating the problem and hope this may help them to tackle it if they know it is there.

A first tentative step in that direction may be to start by considering the uses of Prehistory for World-history. The latter gets its content from the colonial career of Western powers which require Prehistory in its Hegelian sense in order to dignify their dominance over the conquered and the colonized by some semblance of hegemony. For any power that aspires after such hegemony—and all liberal-imperialist states do—must either exploit the precolonial past of the subject population directly for purposes of empire building or process it by rewriting to serve the same end in more sophisticated ways. The British are exemplary in this respect, for they tried both in India. The past of the "historyless" people they had conquered proved to be extremely useful in their attempt to convert conquest into rulership. The East India Company's fiscal system, judicial institutions, administrative apparatus—cardinal and formative aspects of the colonial state—relied heavily on that past as the primary source of information required to formulate rules and set up structures for governance.[54] Prehistory was, in this case, the clay used by the regime to put itself in shape. But it also provided colonialism with space to install its own versions of the Indian past converting the latter into material for its edifices of colonialist knowledge. It is thus that the "peoples without history" in the subcontinent got history as their reward for subjugation to civilized Europe and World-history, just as elsewhere in realms unredeemably sunken in Prehistory the colonized lacking in footwear and faith got shoes and the Bible.

One of the most outstanding achievements of British power in the East was indeed the production and propagation of colonialist historiography. It was cultivated on Prehistory's vacant plots. What was sown for seed came directly out of post-Enlightenment European and particularly English historical literature packaged for use in Indian schools and universities. The product was history written by Indians themselves in faithful imitation of the Western statist model. Unknown to Hegel, India had already been smuggled into World-history by the colonial state for which he had no place in any of his so-called stages, presumably because it did not fit the grand design. But, ironically, Indian authorship did nothing to recover the historicality discarded as Prehistory. Incorporated in World-history, the Indian past continued to be written as a history turning on the colonial and, since Independence, the postcolonial state as its axis.

If World-history has not only penetrated the realm of Prehistory but continues to flourish there, as it does in India and elsewhere in the colonial world by having its statist essence nationalized or indigenized, this is because there is something about the modern Western state-system that must historicize the past on its own terms wherever it operates. In the process the prose of the world loses ground and historicality shrinks in scope to enable a narrowly constructed historiography to speak for all of history. Insofar as such reductiveness is a defining feature of historical narratives produced by the colonized themselves, it shows how well they have been schooled in metropolitan historiography. For the triumph of the state, a Western phenomenon celebrated by philosophy, followed the routes of commerce and conquest to annex the continents of Prehistory intellectually as well. The complicity between imperialism and World-history is therefore not merely a question of the expropriation of the pasts of the colonized by colonizers. It stands also for the globalization of a regional development specific to modern Europe—that is, the overcoming of the prose of the world by the prose of history.

It is a matter of some curiosity that such overcoming has little to do with the state in the *Aesthetics* where, as Hayden White has pointed out, "Hegel elaborates his theory of historical writing itself."[55] Neither the characterizations of prosaic (as against poetical) mentality nor the conditions of historiography, all discussed at length in that work, require a role for the state to translate the prose of the world into the prose of history. However, in the *Lectures on World History*, drafted presumably at about the same time, the state figures as the principal instrument for the development of history and historiography. It is not merely what provides the prose of history with its central theme, but actually helps to produce it. Was this just a matter of compensating for some lacuna in the other text? Or is this evidence of the essentially theological make-up of World-history? Yet, in the *Aesthetics*, the hand of God is far from obvious in the transition from the prose of life to the prose of the world through to the prose of history. Indeed, there seems to be no problem at all about the compatibility of historiography and secular worldhood left to themselves as they are in that work. It is only when they are hitched to a divine plan that the state steps in as the sine qua non for its realization. From a Hegelian perspective the assimilation of history to theology could, of course, be justified as dialectics that help spiritualize the past by endowing it with some sanctity. But its consequence for a historicality determined to remain planted in the human condition appears to be highly problematic. One wonders if that is a dilemma which may be said to have pulled these two great texts—and with them philosophy itself—in opposite directions on the question of the state in the epoch of its ascendancy.

The prose of the world was, as discussed in the previous chapter, an opening up. It was an invitation to all of historicality, that is, to all of man's being in time and his being with others to write itself into that prose and enter it with all the multiplicity and singularity, complexity and simplicity, regularity and unpredictability of such being. The prose of history shuts that out by its exclusive and selective approach to the past. By its concentration on the state as the center of man's place in the world it operates as a strategy of containment. Walled in by the state and its historiography the citizen is cut off from his historicality as a citizen of the world. It is up to us, of course, to try and critically understand the nature and consequences of that containment in order to combat it. But any attempt to develop a critique adequate to the task is bound to fail so long as it remains indifferent to the question how World-history tells its stories. For it is precisely these that the containing wall has for its brick and mortar. Which is why our survey requires the narratology of World-history to be put in a perspective that would allow other narrative modes—those on the other side of the limit—to show up and speak up in the next stage of our argument.

4 Experience, Wonder, and the Pathos of Historicality

On learning to write history—the relation of archai *to concept acquisition—colonialism and the translation of* itihāsa *into history—two paradigms: displacement of one by the other under the impact of World-history—the paradigms distinguished by provenance—the novel as the narrative of experience—the initiative of authors and listeners—*itihāsa *and the Mahābhāratic narrative—the meaning of* itihāsa *and the tradition of recursivity—the* rasa *of wonder in Indian poetics—the question of experience and wonder in Western narratives—Greek* thaumazein *and Indian* adbhutarasa*—the past in narratives of experience and those of wonder—temporality in Hegel's idea of history—the pathos of historicality.*

To return to the question of the limit. We have seen it as a line drawn across historicality. The parts so divided may now be distributed in terms of the Aristotelian definition cited in the first chapter. Inside the limit where "everything is to be found," the everything stands for World-history constituted by the nation-states of Europe, euphemistically called the Germanic realm. Outside, where "there is nothing to be found," the nothing is the region of Prehistory. The lands and peoples settled here by an imperialist philosophy speaking for *Geist* have historicality but no history. The excluded are not ethnic or geographical abstractions. They make up the greater part of humanity with its cultures, literatures, religions, philosophies, and so forth. The philosopher goes through the lot systematically to dig them out one by one and tip them into the wastelands of Prehistory. What is discarded is not only the pasts these so-called historyless people live by in their everyday existence but also the modes adopted by their languages to integrate these pasts in the prose of their respective worlds. In this way World-history has promoted the dominance of one particular genre of historical narrative over all the others. That it has succeeded in doing so speaks well of the clever mixture of force and persuasion by which colonialism has ruled for so long in several continents. Indeed, the strategy has been so effective that the persuaded have gone on to produce their own versions of World-history. They have done so consciously as a rational decision, similar to but on the whole more secular than Hegel's, to reject the alternative representations of the past within their own cultures. The displacement of those alternatives by a modern historiography practiced by the Indians themselves is usually regarded as an impressive measure of the success of education introduced by the Raj in the subcontinent. But can education alone suffice to explain the phenomenon? How could the first Indian historians of the colonial era *learn* to write history if history had been altogether unknown to them prior to the advent of colonialism?

It is no taste for idle speculation that prompts us to ask this question. Its legitimacy derives from a well-known tradition of European epistemology going back to the words with which Aristotle opens the *Posterior Analytics*: "All teaching and all intellectual learning come about from existing knowledge."[1] Taken together with the discussion in the concluding chapter of the work (B19), this implies that in learning something man uses an innate faculty or capacity to grasp a set of starting points or principles corresponding to that thing. These starting points or principles (*archai*) are primary in the sense of being prior to everything else and do not depend on demonstration for their validity.

What are the *archai* that enabled the first generation of Indian intellectuals to acquire a knowledge of the science and craft of history introduced from the West? And how did they make those principles known to themselves? For an answer, one may take a clue from what Aristotle has to say about the learning process.[2] According to him, it is a path that leads to comprehension in four stages with perception as the point of departure. Man is born with the ability to perceive what is accessible to his senses in the external world such as colors and sounds that require no learning on his part to be perceived. Proceeding from simple percepts that stand thus for the immediate present, he retains these at the next stage as the recollection of what has been. He then goes on to repeat it to form a persistent memory that multiplies and deepens into experience. The latter culminates eventually in comprehension, that is, in a "state" of understanding which grasps the single and integral universal informing the many experiences gathered in the process. Learning results thus in concept acquisition.

It follows, therefore, that in learning to write history in the Western manner in spite of their exclusion from World-history, the first Indian historians of the colonial era had acquired its concept by graduating from perception to comprehension. Whether they did so by relying mainly on intuition (as in the instance of Ramram Basu) or on institutionalized education (as in the case of the next generation of intellectuals) is a matter of no little interest. However, in the context of our discussion here it is more important to find out the uses they made of the concept. For to proceed from conceptualization to writing they had to relate the concept to some such *archai* within their own tradition as would match a corresponding set of primitives for Western historiography. These are not far to seek, of course. There is a general agreement that "chronicle" and "story" refer to what Hayden White calls "primitive elements" in the historical account.[3] Etymology lends support to this identification by the near synonymity of expressions which connote the past in many European languages ranging from the older "istoria" and "historia" to the latter-day "histoire" and "history."

The corresponding *archai* in some of the Indic languages would be *ākhyāna* or *kathā* of the genre called *itihāsa*. In the Sanskrit from which it is taken, the latter combines two indeclinables, *iti* and *ha*, with a verbal noun to produce a complex structure. "The word *iti*," says Daniel Ingalls, "functions like quotation marks in English to shift the denotandum from thing to word."[4] He illustrates this shifting or *viparyāsakaraṇa*, as grammarians call it, by the phrase *gauriti*. The substantive *gauḥ* stands for the animal ox, but taken together with the indeclinable it is no more than the expression just mentioned. By the same token, *iti* joins the other *avyaya* or indeclinable *ha* in *itihāsa* to turn something that has been or was (*āsīt*) into what has just been said about it. As the commentary in the *Amarakośa* has it: *iti ha āsīt yatreti itihāsaḥ*. The deixis implicit in this operation enables it, even without quotation marks, to indicate the place of a remote past in its telling. Thus a sense of antiquity may be said to have been absorbed in the phrase by long usage to make *itihāsa* mean a traditional account relayed from generation to generation (*itihāsaḥ purāvṛttam*). Since there is no account that satisfies both of these conditions, namely, tradition (*aitihya*) and succession (*pāraṃparya*), better than the Mahābhārata and the Rāmāyaṇa, those two ancient narratives have come to be acknowledged as epitomes of *itihāsa*. Or, to be more precise, they did so until something happened—that is, until the irruption of World-history.

World-history made its way to the subcontinent as an instrument of the East India Company's colonial project and helped it to set up the Raj. It played a vital role in the material as well as intellectual aspect of empire building: materially, by fabricating an elaborate historicist justification for the Company's fiscal system in the subcontinent and its appropriation of the wealth of the land to finance its trade; intellectually, though rather less successfully, by trying to educate Indians to accept their subjugation under British rule as historical evidence of progress. I have discussed these questions elsewhere at some length.[5] All that need be emphasized in the present context is the complicity of Orientalism in hitching *itihāsa* to World-history. It was as if an imperial imagination had been looking for a name by which to designate history as a graft in the Indian soil and found it in *itihāsa*. The translation was initiated from the English side, for it was the interests of the rulers themselves, an English trading corporation, that prompted it. And here again, as elsewhere throughout the world in the mercantile era, translation followed conquest as an exercise in violence rather than anything like a voluntary exchange between languages in a condition of political neutrality. That would go some way to explain the reticence with which the Company's own employees among the pandits of Fort William College greeted the assimilation of *itihāsa* to the vocabulary of World-history. Although Carey had been quick to identify Ramram Basu's work as "history," Mrityunjoy Bidyalankar's *Rajabali*, a narrative of much wider scope published seven years later, found no use for the word *itihāsa* at all.[6] The rulers had modernized the latter, but their subjects were not impressed. Yet there was to be a sea change within less than three decades. Ramkamal Sen's *Dictionary* (1834) has about a dozen entries for "history" and its derivatives in English. The corresponding phrases in Bangla denote "story" in one form or another for all the lexemes, six of which have *itihāsa* in both its traditional and modern sense for synonym.[7]

The graft had obviously taken root even as Hegel was holding forth about the unredeemable historylessness of India. This was an achievement to make colonialism proud irrespective of the flag under which it carried on its trade or fought its wars. And the British, the foremost of empire builders of that age, were justified in writing it into schoolbooks as an outstanding success of their civilizing mission. That mission was, we know, a package made up of the Bible, soap, and history carried by the West to the lands it had conquered. The subcontinent had already been treated to its share of the first two, and now it got history as well. India was launched decisively on its way to civilization. The translation of history as *itihāsa* culminated thus in the triumph of the historicizing process that had begun in South Asia with the East India Company's accession to Diwani not long after the Battle of Plassey.

Translation is notorious for generating ambiguity. For slippages occur in the course of transfer from one language to another, and do so with comic effect sometimes, as in the present instance. The rendering of "history" as *itihāsa* was construed by a section of the Hindu conservative intelligentsia as evidence that India, too, had a historiography of the world-historical kind as old as the Mahābhārata and the Rāmāyaṇa, and the West had at last come to acknowledge this for a fact. There is a play on words behind this claim. Those two epics are known as *purāṇetihāsa*, a compound which allows *itihāsa* to be identified as *purāṇa*, that is, as a discourse made up of traditional accounts going back to antiquity. However, *purāṇa* happens also to be the generic name of the corpus of mythic literature in Sanskrit and, by extension, myths. So the Orientalist translation dovetailed neatly with an ancient collocation to produce a large body of writings that sought to recast Hindu mythology as history. The funny side of this exercise and the guffaws with which it was greeted in its heyday during the decades between the last quarter of the nineteenth century and the First World War must not be allowed to take away from its importance as a modernist project. It had chronology, causality, comparability—indeed, all the method and craft of Western historiography for its equipment. What is equally significant is that it was modernist not in methodology alone but in concept as well. For to be world-historical was to catch up with modernity and its most advanced column, Europe itself, on the road to progress.

But there were others amongst the middle-class Indians themselves who did not find it necessary to step all the way back to antiquity in order to rush ahead into World-history. Educated in the colonial schools, they had learned to accept history as an entirely modern and Western kind of knowledge about the past historicized by writing. If they, too, were caught up in the drift of ambiguity, this had less to do with exchanges between the languages of the East and the West than with the semantics of European languages themselves. Hegel addressed this problem in a comment on the overlapping meanings of *Geschichte*, the German word for "history." Thus,

> in our language, the word [*Geschichte*] combines both objective and subjective meanings, for it denotes the *historia rerum gestarum* as well as the *res gestae* themselves, the historical narrative and the actual happenings, deeds, events—which, in the stricter sense, are quite distinct from one another. But this conjunction of the two meanings should be recognised as belonging to a higher order than that of mere external contingency: we must in fact suppose that the writing of history and the actual deeds and events of history make their appearance simultaneously, and that they emerge together from a common source.[8]

The "higher order" refers, of course, to providential design, and the "common source" to the state. Providentially or not and without the benefit of statehood—Hegel had no room for the colonial state in his scheme anyway—the intellectuals of South Asia had come to grasp the "conjunction of the two meanings" and, unknown to him, started producing the typically modern prose of history. By collapsing the past with its "happenings, deeds, events" into the narrative present, they emulated the West in their writings. Historicality was actualized by being placed under the sign of simultaneity, the "now" that they had come to recognize as the temporal hallmark of modernist representation. Thus India was rescued from Prehistory by her own historians and ushered by them across the border into World-history. This was a momentous crossing. Viewed from one side of that border, it was a passage from myth to history, from fantasy to reason. Viewed from the other side, it could be seen as a shift from a particular paradigm of storytelling to another. If we hesitate to call this a generic shift, it is primarily because the developments that concern us refer a long way back to the *archai* before the formation of genres. Furthermore, we believe that the interaction of concept and practice in a paradigm understood in the Kuhnian sense may help us to grasp the dynamics of the story in terms of its telling rather than in those of its place in a generic table.

Whether the two paradigms had a common origin is a matter of speculation for which we don't have much use in the present context. Suffice it to recall that each had come to establish itself as a recognizably distinct narrative formation at a remote past as old as the older civilizations of East and West and run parallel to each other for centuries as the European "story" and the Indian *itihāsa* until the former, in its role as World-history, assimilated the latter. What did that mean for historicality in its relation to historiography? We shall proceed now to consider that question in the light of what distinguished the two paradigms in the first place. Here it would have been convenient to start our inquiry at the point of their divergence. But that, alas, is hidden in the mists of time. Happily, however, their convergence closer to our own age and the staple of much modern scholarship offers us a retrospective view of the story's development and its culmination in the form most familiar to us as the novel.

The novel is the quintessential narrative of experience. There is no difference of opinion on this point amongst the historians of literature. "Implicit in the novel form in general," writes Ian Watt, there is "the premise, or primary convention, that the novel is a full and authentic report of human experience."[9] In his view, the first modern English novelists like Richardson and Defoe accepted this convention "very literally," as witness, for instance, the latter's use of an autobiographical form for his narrative. This was "as defiant an assertion of the primacy of the individual experience in the novel as Descartes's *cogito ergo sum* was in philosophy," says Watt.[10] Bakhtin agrees but traces the primacy of experience a long way back to the era of Hellenism when the epic had already been novelized. Even at that incipient stage the novel was "determined by experience," according to him. "At its core lay personal experience."[11] The same could be said of history as well, perhaps because historians "tend to be naive storytellers."[12] The very first among them in the West, Herodotus and Thucydides, wrote from experience—one from what he saw and heard in the course of his travels abroad, and the other from what he witnessed nearer home. Authors of what Hegel calls "original history," they belong, according to him, "to the class of historians who have themselves witnessed, experienced and lived through the deeds, events and situations they describe."[13]

To place experience at the heart of a narrative is to stake out a claim to truth in the name of realism and vraisemblance for the novel, and that of authenticity and veracity for historiography. In either case, it is the narrator's testimony that is under scrutiny. A reader satisfied with the "evidence" will sometimes speak of an author approvingly in the language of a judge or jury, as Hazlitt does of Richardson and Lamb of Defoe.[14] But in case of doubt even Herodotus, "the father of history," could end up denounced as "the father of all liars."[15] However, what is involved in the centrality of experience is not only a narrative's claim to truth. It also confers on the narrator the authority of beginning: as author, it is for him to initiate what he can call *his* story. Who initiates the story is an important question. Edward Said, who has formulated it for us and made us aware of its implications for the novel, insists on its cultural specificity. There are cultures, he says, citing Arabic literature as an example, where the question may have no relevance at all; or it applies in ways that are not quite the same as in the West.[16] But it does apply to India where the advent of World-history led to the production of historiography as well as the novel.[17] For, thanks to the impact of colonial rule, life in the subcontinent was not wanting in that incompleteness—Lukács would call it dissonance—which novelization requires. But even for the earlier period when the Western story and Indian *itihāsa* ran on parallel lines, the question of beginning has its uses for our inquiry into their paradigmatic distinctions. It helps us to understand how they differed in their provenance.

We have noticed that the story, as history and novel, had come to be placed under the regime of personal experience during the Hellenic era and issued decisively since then from the storyteller's initiative in the West. Not so in India. There the story, or *kathā*, owed its inauguration primarily to the listener's demand. This emerges clearly from the Mahābhārata. In the form this epic has come down to us, it dates from a time somewhere between 200 B.C. and A.D. 200, but the original is believed to have been much older. The greatest of the *itihāsa* genre of narratives, it has proved to be the most enduring influence on storytelling throughout the ages in South Asia. Consequently its structure of tales within tales, relays of many different voices, an arterial movement which digresses ever so often into loops that rejoin the trunk sooner or later—these and other salient aspects have been the subject of much scholarly discussion since the early nineteenth century. But in all this it is the storyteller who has the pride of place. It is generally assumed, without too many questions asked, that the story flows directly from his initiative. Whether this is owing to an Orientalist imperative to assimilate him to the Homeric bard or, for that matter, to the latter-day European novelist anticipating the providential assimilation of *itihāsa* to World-history, it is difficult to tell. Whatever that may be, it can claim little support from the text.

The scene of narration is clearly laid out in the first book (*ādi-parva*) of the Mahābhārata. A ritual event is in progress at a settlement in the Naimiṣa forest. It is a *satra*, or large-scale sacrifice, that will go on for twelve years and features routines and activities of many different kinds. The host is a Brahmin called Śaunaka who is the *kulapati*, or head of a dominant lineage group in the locality, as the designation suggests. Indeed, a *kulapati* happens, in most cases, to be a local big man, usually a priest and teacher by profession, hence Brahmin by caste, who is also affluent enough to provide food and gifts for a large gathering of guests. Naturally fellow Brahmins turn up in great numbers on such occasions. They do so not only to benefit from potlatch but also out of a sense of kinship and neighborly obligation to help with the numerous chores necessary for so protracted and elaborate a ceremony. There is a lot to do from dawn to dusk, and yet life in such a ritual community is not all drudgery. There are intervals for rest and entertainment as well. That is when the officiants get to know their visitors and interact with them in leisure activities.

The story of the Mahābhārata begins with the arrival of one such visitor. The Brahmins recognize him straightaway as Ugraśravā, son of a well-known storyteller and an able practitioner of the craft himself. So they gather around him hoping to be regaled. But formalities come first. He greets them with folded hands in the usual gesture of obeisance and says a few words to indicate his concern for their spiritual well-being. They take their seats, and Ugraśravā follows to his, as allocated, presumably in accordance to his relatively lower caste status. And after he has had some rest and looks reasonably comfortable, one of the dignitaries makes the first move to request a story, but does so with circumspection. We are not far from a beginning here. An initiative is about to emerge from the listeners' side, as the text makes clear. One of the holy men, it says, intends to ask some questions soliciting a round of stories (*athāpṛcchadṛṣistatra kaścit prastāvayan kathāḥ*), but all he can manage in obvious hesitation is something like "Where are you coming from, Mr. Bard? Where have you been all this time?" (*kuta āgamyate saute kva cāyam vihṛtastvayā kālaḥ*).[18]

The bard understands, of course, what it is all about, but is in no hurry to oblige. Convention requires him to be circumspect as well. He has to be asked. Indeed, he will soon have a few things to say about tradition precisely on this point. He will tell his audience how Vyāsa, the first narrator of the Mahābhārata story, had to be asked by King Janamejaya a thousand times (*sahasraśaḥ*) before delegating his pupil Vaiśampāyana to recite. And even then the latter would expect to be requested again and again (*codyamānaḥ punaḥ punaḥ*) before consenting to narrate it for the king and his retinue of brahmins on a ceremonial occasion like the present one (*MBh* 1.1.56–58). So our young storyteller does his own bit of holding back, as prescribed, but leaves chinks in his reticence large enough to stimulate curiosity. He responds to his interlocutor simply by saying that he has been on a pilgrimage wandering from one sacred place to another across the country. However, what he takes care to mention as well is a cycle of stories he has heard during his travels. Known collectively as the Mahābhārata, it was all about a war fought way back in antiquity between the Pāṇḍavas and the Kurus at Samantapañcaka, a station on the pilgrims' circuit that he has visited himself. The hint is not lost on the audience. Given a choice of puranic tales, religious accounts, and histories of princes and sages, the would-be listeners settle promptly for the Mahābhārata.

The story is at last on its way. Henceforth it will unfold in a retelling that works closely with its listeners as a conversational process. Called *kathāyoga* in the text (*MBh* 1.4.3), that process requires the bard to consult his audience about their preferences not only at the start of the narrative cycle but all throughout. At the end of an episode he will leave it to them to advise what they want to hear next, and an interlocutor who speaks for them will name an event or personality or sometimes even a moral or metaphysical topic around which to spin the next round of tales. Each of the principal narrators of the Mahābhārata has an interlocutor: Ugraśravā has his Śaunaka, Vaiśampāyana his Janamejaya, and Sañjaya his Dhṛtarāṣṭra.

It is not unreasonable perhaps to think of these interlocutors as the *ārambhakāḥ*—literally, initiators—mentioned by Patañjali in his *bhāṣya* on P1.4.29: *ākhyātopayoge*. Kaiyaṭa describes them in his commentary, the *Pradīpa*, as persons distinguished by their "cultivated interest" (*ārambhakā yatnena pravṛttimantaḥ*). Nāgeśa, another commentator, speaks of them as *mukhyāḥ*, or connoisseurs. The *ārambhaka* is thus defined entirely in terms of his taste for and understanding of the performing arts. This makes sense in the context of the discussion on *upayoga*, or usefulness, which is at the heart of P1.4.29. It justifies Pāṇini's ruling in favor of the ablative case-ending (*apādana*) for the source of communication where the utility in question is of a higher order (*prakarṣagati*), such as what is involved in the study of a text under a teacher, and generally the pursuit of learning in a disciplined way (*niyamapūrvakaṃ vidyāgrahaṇam*). It seems to be the grammarians' view that, by contrast, no such discipline is required of the listeners in being entertained by a storyteller (*granthika*) or an actor (*naṭa*). Consequently the latter's performance ranks somewhat lower on the scale of utility and needs no *apādana*.

In other words, the sutra calls for a certain judgment of values, and the commentators make their point by assessing the usefulness of the discipline of learning favorably in comparison to that of the cultivation of taste in the performing arts. It is important for their argument, therefore, to highlight the range and quality of the *ārambhaka*'s aesthetic competence and not his *function* as a listener, which is what concerns us. For our understanding of that function we rely on the Amarakośa to translate *ārambha* as commencement or introduction, hence *ārambhaka* as the initiator who helps a recital of stories to begin. Acknowledged by the others in an audience as the most knowledgeable and cultured among them, he negotiates on their behalf the choice of stories to be told. Which is why the interlocutors, assigned to that role, figure in the Mahābhārata as more than decorative details. As *ārambhakas* they have a strategic function in gathering the listeners' will in the development of the narrative cycle and presenting it at the inauguration of each of its episodes (*upākhyāna*).

It is thus that provenance makes for a clear distinction between the two paradigms: in the West the narrative issues from the narrator's initiative, in South Asia from the listener's. This corresponds to yet another set of distinctions that bear critically upon the question of experience. Its primacy in the long European tradition of storytelling from the Hellenic *historie* to the modern novel has already been noticed. But this is conspicuous for its absence in the Indian case. Here it is a certain distance between narrator and event rather than the immediacy of any personal experience that makes up the story for *itihāsa*. The distancing is done by a verb acting closely together with two indeclinables (*avyaya*) to form that word. Compounded as *itiha* they point out what is said about a past by enclosing it in invisible quotation marks, as Ingalls has observed.[19] Like all quotation marks the function of the compound is to keep the utterance apart from the speaker, the storyteller from the story, as if to put it beyond doubt that it is really not *his* story. In other words, his role in the telling is not that of a witness but a reporter. This applies even to the so-called eyewitness accounts of the Kuru-Pāṇḍava war. We have no direct access to what Sañjaya, who is supposed to have seen it all, actually said as he described it, blow by blow, to the blind king Dhṛtarāṣṭra. The version we have in the Mahābhārata is what has come down to us as told by a long succession of raconteurs from Vyāsa to Ugraśravā. Which makes it all very secondhand with no room in it for anything like direct experience.

The idea of distantiation is emphasized further by the verb. Based on the radical √*as* it may be taken to mean "to be" and lead to the interpretation given in the *Padamañjarī*, that is, *iti ha āsīt iti yatrocyate sa itihāsaḥ*, or as rendered roughly in English, "*Itihāsa* is where the statement 'This is how it was or has been' belongs." The *Amarakośa*, mentioned earlier, says the same thing and varies only slightly to read *yatreti* for *yatrocyate*. What is important to note is that both have *yatra*, meaning "where," to locate *itiha* with all that it stands for in *itihāsa*. The latter emerges from this formulation thus as a discursive site where *itiha* deposits whatever is enclosed in it as citable about the past. But who does the depositing? We have some guidance on this point from Kaiyaṭa as he explains Patañjali's use of the phrase *aitihāsikaḥ pourāṇikaḥ* in his *bhāṣya* on P4.2.60. To cite the *Pradīpa*,

> The word *itiha* belongs to the tradition of *upadeśa* [which may be taken to mean, in English, instruction, advice, or informa-

tion] that has been handed down. *Itiha* has been posited in this, whence *itihāsa*.

(*aitihāsika iti. itihaśabda upadeśapāramparye vartate. iti hāsyate asminniti itihāsaḥ.*)

It is clear that unlike the lexicographers Kaiyaṭa relies for his interpretation on the verb *asyate* based on the same root √*as*, but taken in its alternative meaning "to throw," or as Nāgeśa has it in his *Udyota*, "to posit or place." We follow him in our reading of Kaiyaṭa to say that it is the tradition of teaching or simply telling stories (*ākhyāna*) which has posited *itiha* in *itihāsa*.

Itihāsa as the repository of the tales told by tradition and bequeathed from one generation to the next since antiquity has little to do with the immediacy of experience. To the contrary, recursivity rules, as in the Mahābhārata, the most outstanding example of the genre. Everything in this epic is an exercise in retelling. Even the very first narrator tells it as told by his guru, Vyāsa. It is hard to improve on that as an instance of repetition. As for the audience, the stories they want to hear are stories they have already heard. In fact, there are numerous occasions when the storyteller is asked to follow up the shorter version of an episode immediately by a more elaborate one. And this is not a matter of any individual listener's caprice. Convention allows *itihāsa* to be narrated in abridgement as well as at length, and one is as good as the other (*iṣṭaṃ hi viduṣāṃ loke samāsavyāsadhāraṇam*; *MBh:Ādiparva* 1.1.49). Indeed, the problem of choice between the competing attractions of experience and repetition is settled in the opening verses of the Mahābhārata. A traveler, who is also a professional storyteller, arrives after a long pilgrimage. Nobody shows any interest at all in his tales of the road. On the contrary, they dip eagerly into his repertoire of stories already told. A scene, less Western and more Indian, is not easy to imagine.

But what do the listeners get out of all this? This is a question in which experience seems to have been already assumed to be the only possible source of novelty for a story. However, the fact that the Mahābhārata audience did not look up to personal experience alone to produce interesting stories for them might have been due, arguably, to a very different idea of novelty altogether. What that was may be gathered from the murmur of a few old words still left in the text. It has survived age, amnesia, and sectarian redaction to remind us of a faith in the story's ability to renew itself in retelling. The listeners expect to hear *citrāḥ kathāḥ* (*MBh* 1.1.3)—literally, tales of wonder—and yet opt happily for the familiar stories of the Mahābhārata. If they see no contradiction in this, is it because they have come to trust a narrative to generate wonder, the ultimate form of novelty, by repetition? Let us consider the keywords, *wonder* and *repetition*, in this context.

The sense of wonder is conveyed in Sanskrit by a cluster of nearly synonymous words listed together in the *Amarakośa* (1.7.19), the most authoritative lexicon of the language. These are, apart from *citra* mentioned above, *vismaya*, *adbhuta*, and *āścarya*. They all occur in the epic from time to time to indicate the quality and manner of narration and response evoked. There is a peculiarity about one of them, as pointed out by Pāṇini.[20] This is the formation *āścarya* in which the affix *yat*, added to the radical √*car*, combines with the preposition *ā* and the augment *suṭ* to mean something that is *anitya*, or "unusual." Take the augment out and it will turn into the antonym *ācarya* meaning a conduct to be "prescriptive," "habitual," or "usual," that is, predictable, hence the very opposite of wonder. The semantic inversion brought about thus by grammar holds for the other terms of the series as well. Prized out of the usual, *adbhuta* and *vismaya*, too, have earned a distinctive place for themselves in the vocabulary of Sanskrit poetics.

Wonder, or *adbhuta*, is one of eight (some say nine) principal elements of traditional Indian aesthetics. Traditional does not mean premodern in this case. Much of this tradition interacts with and thrives in Indian art and literature even today. Yet in discussing *itihāsa* prior to its convergence with World-history it is important to avoid anachronism and keep in mind the thinking that culminated in the tenth-century works on aesthetics by Ānandavardhana and Abhinavagupta and continued to influence narratology for the greater part of the next millennium until the beginning of colonial rule. Staying close to that tradition, let us refer to the aesthetics of wonder by its Sanskrit name, *adbhutarasa*, that is, the *rasa* of wonder.

Rasa is the soul of poetry, and generally the essence of aesthetic response. If we hesitated to use the term so far, it was only to avoid the embarrassment of translation. For the word is truly untranslatable, and there is no writer on the subject who does not say so. One of the most eminent of them, Sushil Kumar De, speaks for all commentators when he observes thus:

> It may be pointed out here that [the] subtle conception of Rasa makes it difficult to express the notion properly in Western critical terminology. The word has been translated etymologically by the terms "flavour," "relish," "gustation," "taste," "Geschmack," or "saveur"; but none of these renderings seems to be adequate. The simpler word "mood," or the term "Stimmung" used by Jacobi may be the nearest approach to it, but the concept has hardly any analogy in European critical theory.[21]

For our purpose we shall use the simpler term *mood* or *attunement* (borrowing from the German *Stimmung*) interchangeably with *rasa* and call *adbhutarasa* the mood of wonder. Astonishment, or *vismaya*, goes with it as an "abiding emotion" (*sthāyibhāva*) to serve for its base. Together they constitute the category of wonder in the *rasa* system. This does little, of course, to overcome the difficulty of translation. To the contrary, it highlights the untranslatability of the Mahābhāratic cycle in terms of the Western narrative paradigm. For experience, which lies at the core of the latter, according to Bakhtin, has no place in *adbhutarasa*.

Experience stands for truth in the European narrative. Since the beginning of historicization and novelization, its value as truth has come to be identified and assessed as a function of its immediacy. The less mediated an experience is in time and space, the truer it is. That is what makes the self so important for the representation of experience in history and the novel. Since, as Gadamer points out, "Everything that is experienced is experienced by oneself," the advantage of a "definite immediacy" combines in the experiencing self with that which accrues from the unifying function of recollection.[22] Which is why the autobiographical is so conspicuous for the attention it receives in the genealogies of the European narrative. For nothing is more immediately and comprehensively related to the latter than its narrator. Any story attested by him as a witness will be regarded as a claim to truth. Whether the attestation comes in the historical mode of Herodotus or the fictional mode of Defoe makes no difference, for even the verisimilar with its air of truth is no less true than the actual. In either case, its truthfulness must be subjected to a test in which the relation between what is said in the story and how it is said has to be examined, following tradition, in the light of Aristotle's idea of truth as a sort of resemblance between a thing and the soul's experience of it, or Aquinas's notion of a thing's correspondence to the intellect, or Kant's formulation about "the agreement of knowledge with its object," and so forth. In this way, experience, which brings the world into the narrative, keeps the narrative firmly beholden to the world.

Even the Western tale of wonder is entangled in the logic of such externalization. It, too, is tethered to experience, and yet what experience brings to that genre from its encounter with the world is not knowledge but its frustration. It is out there chasing things all the time but does not understand what it sees. All it can do is report on the difference between expectation and actuality. In other words, the work of experience is entirely privative in this case, although that does not stop its narratives from being subjected in their turn to tests of verification no less severe than those mentioned above. Stephen Greenblatt reflects on this irony in his well-known study of marvels:

> The expression of wonder [he writes] stands for all that cannot be understood, that can scarcely be believed. It calls attention to the problem of credibility and at the same time insists upon the undeniability, the exigency of the experience.[23]

The problem of credibility is so acute here precisely because the correspondence between knowledge and its object, between intellect and the thing it wishes to grasp, could not be more wanting than it is in such experience. And yet the pursuit of things goes on, the pursuit of novelty for its own sake. Driven by a desire for the particular, which always gives it the slip, it is an inquisitive, homeless, restless phenomenon easily recognizable as curiosity. As such, it stands far apart from genuine wonder, which knows how to contemplate the world and by contemplating understand it.

Martin Heidegger, who insists on this distinction between curiosity and wonder, does so in order to reinvest the latter with some of the sense of contemplation given in the ancient Greek word *thaumazein*.[24] He construes it as "disposition," an Aristotelian term taken from the *Metaphysics* (Δ.19.1022b1). In that text it stands for "some kind of position" articulated in parts "either by place or capacity or form."[25] Heidegger translates it as *Befindlichkeit*, which also means attunement. It refers not only to a position but focuses on the moment of positing to indicate how one is to find oneself positioned or disposed. Understood thus, certain aspects of a long lost European tradition show up in the light of an unmistakable affinity with the ancient Indian concept of wonder.

We say so taking a cue from Walter Benjamin's reading of Herodotus, believed to have been the first Western historian to rely on the immediacy of experience for his accounts of the past. Benjamin, however, calls him "the first storyteller of the Greeks" and refers to his narrative of a victory celebration in which the Persian king Cambyses subjects the defeated king Psammenitus of Egypt to public humiliation. It is a moving scene that shows how the royal captive looks on without flinching as his daughter is forced to march past dressed as a maidservant and his son led to execution, but breaks down when he sees one of his servants, a poor old man, being escorted in a file of common prisoners. Benjamin observes that the story, though told in the "driest" manner, is capable of several different interpretations apart from one we owe to Montaigne. For "Herodotus offers no explanation" and leaves the story free to relate itself to the listener's sentiment and judgment—and to his sense of wonder. "That is why," writes Benjamin, "this story from ancient Egypt is still capable after thousands of years of arousing astonishment and thoughtfulness. It resembles the seeds of grain which have lain for centuries in the chambers of the pyramids shut up air-tight and have retained their germinative power to this day."[26]

If "the father of history" in the West could also be called "the first storyteller" and some of his stories found capable of "arousing astonishment and thoughtfulness," it speaks not only of a convergence between history and story at some point upstream in the European tradition, but also of a parallelism between the ancient Greek *thaumazein* and the ancient Indian *adbhuta*. What they have in common is a certain indifference to the immediacy of experience. Heidegger rejects the notion of people being "displaced *into* these or those dispositions by 'getting' them" as a part of some "lived experiences." It works the other way around, according to him. "In truth," he writes, "it is the disposition that displaces us, displaces us into such and such a relation to the world, into this or that understanding or disclosure of the world, into such and such a resolve or occlusion of one's self, a self which is *essentially* a being-in-the-world."[27] Consequently wonder has little use for experience insofar as it is a disposition that puts us in a particular relation to the world. To a large extent this is true of *adbhuta*, too, as an attunement, that is, as a *rasa*. A far cry from curiosity and all that it stands for, it is clearly disengaged from experience, as Abhinavagupta, the principal writer on *rasa* theory insists.[28]

It is his view that aesthetic response is neither a relation of perception to its object nor an objective entity nor an effect related to some cause or vice versa. The usual means of our access to experience, such as inference (*anumāna*) and memory, have no role in this response. Indeed, the apprehension of *rasa* is nothing if not mediated. Which is why even the representation of grief, he argues citing some tragic episodes of the Rāmāyaṇa, involves no grieving on the part of narrators or actors or their audience. Had that been otherwise, the story of Rāma and Sīitā, with all its sadness, would never have been told or staged. As it happens, its impact on listeners and spectators is not one of distress but an uplifting kind of joy. This is true of the entire range of *rasas*, but more so of *adbhuta* than perhaps any other if only because the joy of wonder is germane to all of them. The eminent Italian scholar, Raniero Gnoli, explains it thus:

> According to Abhinavagupta and his school, this wonder is present, in a broader sense, in every form of life, it is like consciousness itself, the element which distinguishes consciousness or spirit from inanimate matter. Aesthetic sensibility, as Abhinava says, is nothing but a capacity of wonder more elevated than the ordinary one. An opaque heart does not wonder. . . . The appearance of the beautiful does not arouse in it any shock (*kṣobha*) or wonder.[29]

This very heightened joy of wonder, characteristic of *adbhuta*, is known in Indian aesthetics as *camatkāra*. An ancient word, it is usually rendered in English as "supernormal rapture." Why supernormal? Because it exceeds all ordinary mental states. Disengaged from experience, it does not claim to produce anything out of a given set of causes nor inform anybody of objects attainable by the common means of knowledge. Neither productive nor informative by intention, it is still a knowledge in the most profound sense of the term. For the apprehension of *rasa* is indistinguishable from self-knowledge, and the rapture generated by *camatkāra* or wonder approaches *ānanda*, the most profound state of spiritual bliss.

It is in this sense that *itihāsa* is a narrative of wonder. It is not tied to any particular experience and exhausted, therefore, by retelling. The question has been discussed by Abhinavagupta at some length with reference to the Rāmāyaṇa.[30] Commenting on a point made in Bharata's *Nāṭyaśāstra*, he says that the story of Rāma can never be reproduced, although it can be re-narrated and re-perceived as it often is. The moments of repetition, which he insists on distinguishing from each other in this context, are *anukaraṇa*, *anukīrtana*, and *anuvyavasāya*, translated by Gnoli, respectively, if not quite elegantly, as reproduction, re-narration, and re-perception. To think of a recitation of that story or any of its episodes as a reproduction would be a logical absurdity, according to Abhinavagupta. For we take something to be a reproduction or copy (*amukhya*) by checking it against the original, against that of which it is a copy (*mukhya*).[31] But where is the original in this case? No one in an audience (nor a spectator at a dramatic representation) has ever had a firsthand knowledge by which to verify whatever he was told about the eponymous hero. Nor did any storyteller have anything but the last heard version of the story for his authority. In other words, there has been no experience to validate the claim of this cycle of *itihāsa* stories as an authentic reproduction of some lived past. Rather, it is the retelling of what has been told many times and the re-perception—should we say, re-audition—of what has once been heard that gives this kind of narrative its distinction. However, the once-told and once-heard is never the same when repeated next time. The once-again is separated from each previous instance by an irreducible hiatus, which would continue to generate variations, and with them wonder, at every retelling.

There are obvious implications of this poetics for some of the fundamental questions of literature, such as those about the general and the particular, the real and the verisimilar, the individual and the typical, and so forth. A great deal has been written on such matters in works on Indian aesthetics, especially in those by the theoreticians of the Dhvani school. Our own interest leads us in another direction to explore the problem of historicality in the narratives of experience and wonder. What is at issue here is the function of the past as it differs from one paradigm to the other. *Itihāsa*, true to etymology, has the past as its essence. But it is a past anchored to no experience in particular. It is precisely such indefiniteness and openness that enables it to produce, as we have seen, an infinite number of stories and the latter to generate wonder without end. The absence of closure helps also to extend the realm of wonder beyond myth and fantasy. Unlike what Western fantasy about the Oriental and the exotic makes it out to be, there are numerous tales of this genre which have their scenes set firmly in the secular and the quotidian. Yet, if they have proved to be an inexhaustible source of wonder for their audience, it is only because they allow language to illuminate what is unusual about the usual in everyday life. There is no reason why they should not be acknowledged as the stuff that constitutes a broad and comprehensive historicality. But no such acknowledgment has been forthcoming, for World-history, with its discourse modeled on the narrative of experience, has other ideas about the past.

The tale of wonder lives happily with the past. Indeed, the relationship of time and story there is one of playfulness, each renewing the other in the course of an interaction that can never end if only because it has never been tied to a beginning. But it is a different matter when it comes to the narrative of experience. The latter relates to the past only in terms of a perpetual tension. However, the manner in which that tension expresses itself varies significantly between the novel and historiography—the two most representative discourses of this genre. The novel, we know, is rooted in experience. This involves, says Bakhtin, "a new way of conceptualizing time."[32] What is new about such conceptualization is the primacy and immediacy of the present in the narrative. The story develops as a contemporary of the storyteller and shares the "now" of his protagonists. In doing so it moves sharply away from what Bakhtin calls the "absolute past," borrowing the term with some modification from Goethe and Schiller.[33] It stands for "the normative attitude towards the epic," which Lukács, following the same authority, characterizes as "an attitude assumed towards something completely in the past." Time in the past is "static and can be taken in at a single glance."[34] Bakhtin, on his part, identifies staticity with tradition as contrasted to "personal experience and the free thought that grows out of it,"[35] and goes on to explain what he believes to be "absolute" about the epic past:

> It lacks any relativity, that is, any gradual, purely temporal progressions that might connect it with the present. It is walled off absolutely from all subsequent times, and above all from those times in which the singer and his listeners are located. . . .
>
> . . .
>
> Precisely because it is walled off from all subsequent times, the epic past is absolute and complete. It is as closed as a circle; inside it everything is finished, already over. There is no place in the epic world for any openendedness, indecision, indeterminacy.[36]

The tension between the past and the narrative of experience could not be more explicitly stated. The novel overcomes the tension by radically breaking away from that past. The prose of history, that is, historiography, does so by more circumspect, one could say almost statesmanly, means as appropriate for so statist a discourse. Circumspection is quite in order, because what is at issue here is a certain idea about the negative aspect of time. "Time," says Hegel, "entails the property of negativity."[37] It is unsparing in its destructiveness. "It seems that all must perish and that nothing endures," he writes, invoking some very familiar nineteenth-century images of fallen grandeur: "Every traveller has experienced melancholy. Who has stood among the ruins of Carthage, Palmyra, Persepolis or Rome without being moved to reflect on the transience of empires and men, to mourn the loss of the rich and vigorous life of bygone ages?"[38]

The fear of transience haunts him at every turn of his thinking on time based as it is on the Aristotelian model of a continuity made up of temporal points, that is, a succession of "nows." However, he is quick to admit that "the point of time proves at once to be its own negation, since, as soon as *this* 'now' is, it supersedes itself by passing into another 'now' and therefore reveals its negative activity."[39] In other words, transience follows necessarily from the flow of time, and since there is no way of stopping it, all that can be done is to mitigate the corrosive impact of negativity by the power of memory.

Memory is basic to Hegel's view of history. But the role assigned to it is protective rather than nurturing. In other words, it is not for memory to hold the past in its womb and let time work on it slowly and creatively until it is ready to be born again in repetition. In Hegel's thinking time relates to the past as an adversary. It destroys everything and the past is not spared, whereas by contrast Mnemosyne, the goddess of memory, has the doors of her temple open to all that survives time's ravages. But the possibility of such survival is itself predicated on the opposition of state to time. Hegel writes of this, in mythic terms, as a contest between Chronos and Zeus. Chronos devours his own children, just as time annihilates everything it brings to life. This myth is not without symbolic meaning, says Hegel:

> For natural life is in fact subjected to time and brings into existence only the ephemeral, just as e.g. the prehistoric age of a

people, which is only a nation, a tribe, but does not form a state or pursue aims that are inherently stable, falls a victim to the unhistorical power of time.[40]

However, Zeus, "the political god," was able to check the power of time and its constant flux. "He did so by creating a conscious ethical institution, i.e. by producing the state."[41] The opposition of state to time turns thus into the opposition of the historical to the unhistorical. Henceforth state and history will need each other. The former stands up to time by institutionalizing itself. This requires what Hegel calls "formal commandments and laws, i.e. general and universally valid directives." But institutionalization alone is no guarantee against the depradation of time. The state remains suspended in "an incomplete present" so long as it is unable to "understand itself and develop an integrated consciousness" in terms of a past. It is the function of history to provide the state with such a past as a record of its development. And historiography serves as the scribe to put the record in writing and make it as enduring as possible. The formal commandments, laws, and directives—indeed, all the principal instruments of its authority and events and deeds associated with it—become intelligible in the light of this record "on which [writes Hegel] Mnemosyne, for the benefit of the perennial aim which underlies the present form and constitution of the state, is impelled to confer a lasting memory."[42]

It is thus that state and historiography came to form the strategic alliance known as World-history in order to overcome the negativity of time. The control of the past is essential to that strategy. Experience lends itself as a useful mechanism of control in this respect. The novel puts it to use by disconnecting it surgically from the absolute past of the epic. But the writing of World-history, the other most important narrative of experience, seeks to control the past by a somewhat different device. Far from severing it from experience, it uses the latter to collect and store the past. It is quite understandable, therefore, that Hegel should open the First Draft of his *Lectures on World History* with a eulogy of the so-called original history as a "written record" of what Herodotus and Thucydides had "themselves witnessed, experienced and lived through." This is how, he says, the historian "fashions a whole out of material from the past," gathers what is scattered, fleeting, and fortuitous, and "sets it up in the Temple of Mnemosyne, thereby investing it with immortal life."[43] Translated in secular terms and seen in its statist context, that makes the Temple of Mnemosyne look pretty much like the Public Record Office.

In the event the battle of paradigms was won for the West. Experience triumphed over wonder, World-history over *itihāsa*. The consequence for storytelling was not only a shift from the listener's initiative to the narrator's, or from a public provenance to one that was private. More significantly, the story, as history, was dislodged from civil society and relocated in the state. William Carey left us with a record of this move when he wrote, "I *got* Ram Boshu [Ramram Basu] to compose a history of one of their kings." We have emphasized the word *got* to show how a pioneering indigenous exercise in the Western mode of writing Indian history had its theme carefully picked by a colonial hand, and it was conceived, appropriately enough, as a statist theme from the sponsor's point of view. But that was also the moment of our admission to World-history. Until then we, "people without history," had been left out in the cold of Prehistory. However, once enfranchised, we outdid our European rulers and teachers in our enthusiasm for the prose of history. The wide open fields of historicality beyond the precincts of statist narrative were all but forgotten by the historians. No one among them paid heed to the alarm sounded once in a while by a creative voice to complain how schooled academic writing on the Indian past had cut itself off from the prose of the world and the stories it had to tell.

One of those who spoke up was Rabindranath Tagore. In a statement made only a few weeks before his death he expressed bitter disappointment about the poverty of historiography. It was, he thought, exclusively concerned with empires and rulers and their public affairs. There could be no place for creative work such as that of a writer in this kind of historical representation. He was forthright in his reproach: "Off with your history," he said.[44] These words affect me with a sadness I find it difficult to overcome. Here is a voice second to none in its authority on such matters, and yet it is a loser's voice. Even the impatience and irritation ring with a sense of defeat. It is not that in speaking up as he did in the very last days of his life the poet was trying to push anything like the agenda for a new historiography. All he intended was perhaps to leave behind him a testament about the pathos of historicality. For it is the latter that has lost out, generating a pathos in every sense of the term as used by Northrop Frye.[45] Weak, inarticulate, and excluded, the prose of the world—historicality's discourse—displays all the symptoms of a low-mimetic tragedy.

We have come to recognize that prose as the narrative of being-with-others and seen how the characteristic moments of its particularity and individuality, complexity and volatility, chance and change tend to cling to the worldhood of being at its grassroots. When it made its debut at the dawn of history it looked as if it might prove to be "the whole breadth of prose in human existence." But the hope of making historicality coextensive with the human condition itself did not materialize. The other prose—the prose of history, that is, historiography powered by statehood—took over and pushed it to the very margins of World-history. Isolated and powerless, it suffers from what Frye calls "the inarticulateness of the victim." Poetry, he tells us, had one of the "great masters of pathos" in Wordsworth. He could make a sailor's mother speak about her dead son in a manner that conveyed the pathos of a "failure of expression."[46] History has not been so lucky. The noise of World-history and its statist concerns has made historiography insensitive to the sighs and whispers of everyday life. Once in a while we have works that show at least some awareness of the problem. However, the solutions offered turn out in most cases to be exercises meant to relieve the dullness of academic history writing rather than address the statist preoccupation, which is what causes that dullness in the first place. Consequently the historicality of the events and sentiments which inform the prose of the world remains unacknowledged.

Finally, a word about exclusion—"the root idea of pathos." It applies as much to the fictional hero as to our subject, historicality. Excluded from World-history, it has shrewdly assimilated itself to the latter's mode of self-representation as historiography—the dominant mode of writing the past. And in doing so, it has inspired the intellectuals of the "peoples without history," who had only recently been admitted to World-history, to emulate the statism of their European mentors. The result has been to produce historical accounts in which the nationalism of the colonized competes with metropolitan imperialism in its bid to uphold the primacy of the state. All the characteristic symptoms of the pathos of exclusion show up in the effort—"a conflict between the inner and outer world," an *alazon* complex so called after "someone who pretends or tries to be something more than he is," and not the least an eagerness to sublimate the effects of an internalized colonization by irony only to get it mired comically in self-pity.

Speaking as one caught up as much as anyone else in the statist predicament of South Asian historiography, I feel that we have not been entirely unaware of the problem. In this we have inherited a concern already apparent, however weakly and unevenly, in a tradition of left-nationalist, Marxist, and generally anti-imperialist writings on Indian history. The projects of feminist, dalit, and subaltern studies reflect that concern. But whether all this has translated adequately in our understanding and practice as historians is not obvious yet. The quality of my own participation in this effort has been part of a common debility in this regard, and I present these observations in the spirit of an autocritique. In doing so, I have taken my stand at the limit in order to gain a critical perspective on the problem. For I believe that to identify and formulate a problem is to take a step towards solving it.

5 Epilogue: The Poverty of Historiography—a Poet's Reproach

Rabindranath Tagore's critique of historiography and his appeal for a return to historicality—childhood experiences of seeing and the inauguration of his own development as a poet—poetic development considered in terms of possibility and its actualization—historicality and facticity—seeing in the second-degree and its role in making the world one's own—an upanishadic statement and its relation to Tagore's critique of historiography—the preoccupation of academic historiography with public affairs of the state and its failure to deal with the phenomenon of creativity—inwardness of the creative process and the question of statism in historiographical representation—history as a narrative concerned with the everyday world.

Rabindranath Tagore, the great Indian writer, is known mainly for his literary works. It is less known that he was a most accomplished historian as well. The Indian past has been thematized in many different ways in his narrative poems, plays, and novels. But it is his essays that testify best to a deep and pervasive sense of history. They impress as much by the range of his scholarship as by the skill with which he deploys it in the argument. Taken together, the essays stand for an original vision distanced no less from the colonialist historiography propagated by the Raj and the ideologues of imperialism than from the narrowly sectarian Hindu view of the past that had been influential in nationalist thought since its formulation by Bankimchandra Chattopadhyay in the 1870s. Tagore overcame his early inclination in favor of the latter to settle eventually on a strong anti-imperialist, secular, and liberal-democratic interpretation of Indian history. This was to serve as a basic source of ideas for the freedom movement in its climactic phase between the two world wars. Both Gandhi and Nehru, as well as their followers, drew profusely on it in order to educate and mobilize the people in the campaigns for independence. One would have expected such a writer, an eminent historian in his own right, to speak well of historiography and its practitioners. But that turned out not to be the case, as made clear by the text we wish to present here in continuation of the argument developed so far. Such presentations amount, of course, to re-presentation and risk losing some of the intentionality of the original in the process. However, that risk is perhaps not so great in this case if only because there is no mincing of matters in what has been said.

Called "Sahitye Aitihasikata"—"Historicality in Literature" would be a fair translation—it is the last article but one of Tagore's prose writings published in the Centenary Edition of his collected works.[1] Dated May 1941, it is an authorized transcription of his comments made in the course of a dialogue. I have checked these details with Professor Sankha Ghosh, the leading authority on Tagore, to make sure that there is no ground for doubt about the authenticity—and, for that matter, finality—of the statement. For the death of the poet, some ten weeks later in August that year, makes it one of the very last things he had to say on the subject. His interlocutor, Buddhadev Basu, was a distinguished representative of the younger generation of modernist writers. For some time, since the 1920s, Tagore had been locked in what seems, looking back, an interminable argument with the modernists on a number of issues concerned with realism. It would not be unreasonable, therefore, to think that history might have been one of the terms of that debate in which differences in attitude towards the past tangled with aesthetic, political, and metaphysical questions to make it a lively exchange. The spontaneity of Tagore's intervention as documented here in its bitter, attacking, and almost cantankerous tone speaks in any case of an ongoing wrangle. Indeed, it is obvious from the force and directness of the opening lines of this last testament of his on the relation of literature to historicality that he had had time—perhaps a lifetime—to think about its central thesis.

> I have heard it said again and again [writes Tagore] that we are guided altogether by history, and I have energetically nodded, so to say, in my mind whenever I heard it. I have settled this debate in my own heart where I am nothing but a poet. I am there in the role of a creator all alone and free. There's little to enmesh me there in the net of external events. I find it difficult to put up with the pedantic historian when he tries to force me out of the centre of my creativity as a poet. Let us go back to the inaugural moment of my poetical career (*kabijiboner go-rakar suchanay*).

The way he speaks of history and historians here is unmistakably hostile. The poet with his creativity stands opposed to them. Yet the passage ends by putting history back on the agenda. It may not be, of course, history understood in quite the same way as does the pedant for whom he has no time. But whatever that may be, the author makes his concern for history obvious by announcing his intention to go back to a *suchana*. That word could mean inauguration or commencement or an indication to disclose what is unknown or not quite explicit yet. Whichever way one takes it, to go back to a *suchana* is to retrace a development to its source and let it show up in its history. In joining issue with the kind of historians he criticizes, Tagore is evidently not interested in taking a stand against history as such but in pleading for a different approach to it.

He proceeds to do so by citing three childhood experiences. He recalls seeing the dew glistening on top of a coconut grove at sunrise, seeing a mass of dark blue clouds gathering in the sky above his ancestral house one afternoon, and seeing a cow licking the back of a foal with the affection reserved usually for her own calf. It was, on each occasion, a matter of seeing in a way Tagore claims to have been uniquely his own. "It is precisely in this that one is a poet," he writes.

But how does such seeing make him a poet when, going by the evidence even of his juvenilia, it will be still some time before he starts writing poetry? For him each of these experiences belongs to "the history of that day" (*sedinkar itihase*), which is perhaps understandable in some broad sense of historicity. But how can it be said to belong to the history of his development as a poet, which is the question at issue here?

What is presupposed in this question is an idea of development as actualization—that is, the idea according to which no development may be said to have begun unless its initial moment is identifiable as an actuality. This applies, of course, to many things assigned by common sense to the order of objective reality. Countable, measurable, quantifiable generally speaking, they have no use for possibility in order to actualize. The real or actual coincides with the possible in them. "Otherwise stated," says Kant, "the real contains no more than the possible. A hundred real thalers do not contain the least coin more than a hundred possible thalers."[2] However, it is quite a different matter when it comes to the kind of reality involved in poetic development, as Tagore seems to indicate by pointing to his childhood experiences.

So far as he is concerned, those experiences belong truly to the history of his growing up as a poet but do so as a possibility. One could think of this, arguably, as a sort of prehistory. However, unlike the prehistory reconstructed from broken shards as a past that is incomplete for want of evidence, what we have here is entirely future-oriented. As such, it requires no evidence of actualization, nor even of a beginning, but simply the recognition of something yet to be. Tagore, his own historian in this article, answers that call for recognition by going back to the *suchana*, the obscure and yet undisclosed source where those experiences are still coiled in the incipience of sheer possibility.

What does a possibility that is merely incipient amount to? It amounts in this instance to tracing the formation of a creative individuality back to its roots in a region of primal experience. But that experience, however primal, is by no means inert. It has a life of its own and a movement characterized by a certain towardness, although towards what is not yet clear. It is, in short, a tendency that does not know where it is going. However, insofar as it is going somewhere at all, it is a movement in time. It is thus a tendency already informed by historicality. By displacing actuality in favor of possibility and situating the inaugural moment of his life as a poet within a mere tendency of the possible, Tagore is projecting historicality into areas beyond the bounds of historiography. For the latter, with its commitment to the objectifying processes it regards essential for any understanding of experience, must have it represented by facts.

Historicality, too, demands facts, especially when it comes to writing about one's own being, that is, when one writes history in the sense that one is that history oneself. The factuality involved in this case is "ontologically totally different from factual occurrence of a kind of stone," says Heidegger. Following a neo-Kantian tradition that goes back to Fichte, but adapting it in his own way, he characterizes this very different order of factuality as facticity. "The concept of facticity," he explains, "implies that an "innerworldly" being has being-in-the-world in such a way that it can understand itself as bound up in its "destiny" with the being of those beings which it encounters within its own world."[3] Unlike the factuality of historiographic representation, the facticity of being must be grasped in advance. It is as if the phenomenon to which it refers has to be apprehended as such before yielding its meaning or indicating its motivation. The tendency acknowledged by Tagore as the prehistory of his being as a poet clearly satisfies this preliminary condition of historicality. Even then it amounts to no more than the facticity of a prelude—the *prastāvanā*, so to say, of ancient Indian dramaturgy that comes between the raising of the curtain and the appearance of actors on the stage.

Prelude or preliminary, the importance of this movement is hard to overestimate. For as foreseeing it is already informed by the sense of what is to be expected of the play or what lies beyond the threshold. In other words, even in the absence of an explicit meaning, it carries the promise of a meaningful future in its towardness. It is destined towards something. This is why Tagore interprets his childhood experiences as signposts directed towards a destination which is that of his self-realization as a poet: "It is in this [seeing] that one is a poet (*kobi je shey eikhanei*)." By that time, at eighty, he had been a poet for all but the first thirteen years of his life, and had summed up the experience of that long encounter with destiny as he wrote, "I am a poet of the world (*ami prithibir kobi*)."[4] Insofar as this was prefigured in an experience of seeing with a child's eye he was keen to have that acknowledged as the initial moment of his historical being as a poet.

For it is in such seeing that he discerns the first steps of his coming out into the world. Whatever in him that was destined to make a poet of him was no longer a mere tendency. It took him gently by the hand and ushered him into his environment so that the latter could open itself up for his innocent gaze to survey. To see not only those scenes mentioned in the article but many others of that kind was for him to experience the world as an outside. He would return to that theme and many of those sights as well in his writings throughout his life. An entire chapter of his autobiography—"Ghar o Bahir" in *Jibansmriti*—written at the midpoint of his career was to be devoted precisely to the attractions of that outside. Reflecting on family disciplines he would write:

> We [the children] were not allowed to go beyond the boundaries of our home. We were not free to circulate even in some parts of the household itself. Which is why I used to look out at the world of nature from behind shutters. There was something there called the outside. It was an infinite extension beyond my reach. And yet its sights, sounds and smells would slip in here and there through chinks in the doors and windows and suddenly touch me. It was as if it were sending out so many signals through the gaps between the bars to engage me in a game. It was the one that was free, while I myself was fettered. There was nothing that could bring us together, which is all the more why the attraction was so strongly felt.[5]

But however strong the attraction may be, the role he assigns himself in this very first scene of his coming out is merely that of a passive partner. It is the outside that beckons him and presents the world for him to see. He has yet to make the world his own, which is precisely what he proceeds to do in an answering gesture as he raises his perception of the world to a second degree. Whatever he sees—the garden, the clouds, the animals, the rivers, the countryside viewed from a boat, or the cityscape from a height—everything that meets his eye is now an object of seeing in a manner he insists is entirely his and his alone. "In the history of that day there was no one other than myself who saw those clouds in quite the same way as I did," he writes. And again, "In the entire history of that day it was Rabindranath alone who witnessed the scene with enchanted eyes." Assertions of this kind occur as a refrain throughout the article to make it clear that seeing is no longer a passive response to the call of the outside. It is now an instrument of appropriation by which the self has made the world its own.

This second-degree seeing serves as a critical link between the being's coming out in the world and its self-realization in a poetic destiny. It has still some way to go before reaching that destination but is heading there all right. For it can claim the world appropriated thus by seeing it as "mine." And in this mineness it has all it needs for its creativity—the images that will distinguish its vision from that of others, the words that will be recognizably different from those produced by other voices. By the same token appropriative seeing provides it also with the material for creatively writing itself into the "history which we ourselves are." It is understandable, therefore, that in opposing this other kind of facticity to the object-historical conventions of historiography Tagore should choose the primal scene of childhood as the site to launch his critique. For it helps him to identify what has already been his ownmost so early in his life and the role it had in structuring the prehistory of his growth and maturation as a writer. By regressing thus from the actual to the possible and projecting the latter on an emergent tendency the poet steps back to the seed-time of an unmediated beginning. It is his way of situating historicality in a paradigm that seeks to deal with the history of creativity at a depth beyond the academic historian (*aitihasik pandit*) to fathom.

The immediacy of that primal sense of grasping the world as one's own has a correlate in the immediacy of the creative process itself. Tagore highlights this by a citation from one of the earlier Upaniṣads, the so-called forest treatises or Āraṇyakas. Compiled over a very long period from around 500 B.C., this body of Indian literature marks the triumph of metaphysics over Vedic ritualism. "A distinct advancement of the claims of speculation or meditation over the actual performance of the complicated ceremonials of sacrifice" and the mythic cosmogonies that informed them, it was the signal of a radical shift, according to Surendranath Dasgupta, the eminent historian of Indian philosophy. In this thinking, he suggests, the idea of the self moves to the center of intellectual and spiritual interest displacing the notion of an external creator. A momentous development in the formation of idealism, it is characterized by Dasgupta as a "change of the mind from the objective to the subjective." However, this change does not involve "any elaborate philosophical discussions or subtle analysis of mind" in the Upaniṣads themselves. It occurs there "as a matter of direct perception, and the conviction with which the truth has been grasped cannot fail to impress the readers."[6] Tagore was one of those readers. Throughout his long career as a writer he drew on that ancient body of teachings about the value of "direct perception" and its truth as an inexhaustible source of ideas, images, stories, and figures of speech for what he had to say about man and God.

It is perhaps the appeal of this directness that leads him to cite one of the earliest, and according to some the most important of the forest discourses—the Bṛhadāraṇyaka—to make the point that he does about the immediacy of the creative process. The passage quoted by him, that is, *na vā are putrāṇāṃ kāmāya putrāḥ priyā bhavantyātmanastu kāmāya putrāḥ priyā bhavanti* (2.4.5), translates thus in English: "It is not for the sake of the sons, my dear, that they are loved, but for one's own sake that they are loved."[7] To understand how Tagore uses these words it may help to read them in context. Part of a dialogue between the sage Yājñavalkya and his wife Maitreyī on the question of immortality, they make up one out of a dozen sentences addressed by husband to wife in a compact passage that reads thus in extenso:

It is not for the sake of the husband, my dear, that he is loved, but for one's own sake that he is loved. It is not for the sake of the wife, my dear, that she is loved, but for one's own sake that she is loved. It is not for the sake of the sons, my dear, that they are loved, but for one's own sake that they are loved. It is not for the sake of wealth, my dear, that it is loved, but for one's own sake that it is loved. It is not for the sake of the Brāhmaṇa, my dear, that he is loved, but for one's own sake that he is loved. It is not for the sake of the Kṣatriya, my dear, that he is loved, but for one's own sake that he is loved. It is not for the sake of worlds, my dear, that they are loved, but for one's own sake that they are loved. It is not for the sake of the gods, my dear, that they are loved, but for one's own sake that they are loved. It is not for the sake of beings, my dear, that they are loved, but for one's own sake that they are loved. It is not for the sake of all, my dear, that all is loved, but for one's own sake that it is loved. The Self, my dear Maitreyī, should be realised—should be heard of, reflected on and meditated upon. By the realisation of the Self, my dear, through hearing, reflection and meditation, all this is known.

Na vā are patyuḥ kāmāya patiḥ priyo bhavati, ātmanastu kāmāya patiḥ priyo bhavati. Na vā are jāyāyai kāmāya jāyā priyā bhavati, ātmanastu kāmāya jāyā priyā bhavati. Na vā are putrāṇāṃ kāmāya putrāḥ priyā bhavanti, ātmanastu kāmāya putrāḥ priyā bhavanti. Na vā are vittasya kāmāya vittaṃ priyam bhavati, ātmanastu kāmāya vittaṃ priyam bhavati. Na vā are brahmaṇaḥ kāmāya brahma priyam bhavati, ātmanastu kāmāya brahma priyaṃ bhavati. Na vā are kṣatrasya kāmāya kṣatraṃ priyaṃ bhavati, ātmanastu kāmāya kṣatram priyaṃ bhavati. Na vā are lokānāṃ kāmāya lokāḥ priyā bhavanti, ātmanastu kāmāya lokāḥ priyā bhavanti. Na vā are devānāṃ kāmāya devāḥ priyā bhavanti, ātmanastu kāmāya devāḥ priyā bhavanti. Na vā are bhūtānāṃ kāmāya bhūtāni priyāṇi bhavanti, ātmanastu kāmāya bhūtāni priyāṇi bhavanti. Na vā are sarvasya kāmāya sarvaṃ priyaṃ bhavati, ātmanastu kāmāya sarvaṃ priyaṃ bhavati. Ātmā vā are draṣṭavyaḥ śrotavyo mantavyo nididhyāsitavyo

Maitreyi, ātmano vā are darśanena śravaṇena matyā vijñānenedam sarvaṃ viditam. (2.4.5)

Now, there is an obvious ambiguity about this passage. The self, it says in the last two sentences, must be realized through hearing, reflection, and meditation. But who or what is this self? *Ātman*, the word for "self," could be read as meaning either the individual self or the supreme self. What is it that it actually refers to—the Puruṣa or the Brahman? The answer divides the two great schools of Indian philosophy—Sāṃkhya and Vedānta. For commentators of the former tendency, the recursive phrase *ātmanastu* is of decisive significance in this respect. They take it to mean "for one's own sake," that is, "for the sake of one's own self," in each of the several instances mentioned here. These individual selves or souls are all alike in their essence and subsumed, according to the Sāṃkhyas, in the Puruṣa, one of the two fundamental principles that govern all being. To know the self in terms of the Puruṣa, they argue, is to know all selves or souls and accede thereby to immortality.

The Vedāntists oppose this view by an alternative reading of the text. Following Śaṅkara's commentaries on the relevant Brahmasūtra (*vākyānvayāt*, 1.4.19), they interpret it in the context of that discussion about immortality between the saintly husband and his wife. He is about to withdraw from the world and retire to the forest, leaving all he owns to his two wives. But one of them is less interested in her share of the property than in knowing how to overcome death. "What am I to do with that which does not make me immortal?" she asks in words unforgettable for their directness and depth: *yenāham nāmṛtā syāṃ kimahaṃ tena kuryāṃ* (2.4.3). His response, in the passage under discussion, is to advise that immortality comes from knowing the Supreme Self and that we must acknowledge our desires as predicated on desire for the latter. He then goes through a list of desirables to demonstrate that they all derive from one's love of the Supreme Self, however different they may be in other respects. The point is clinched in three subsequent passages (2.4.7–9) by a musical analogy to argue that all entities in the universe merge in the Brahman irrespective of variations in genus and species, just as a piece of music played on percussion, wind, and string forms an integral sound, differences in notes and beats notwithstanding. Thanks to a somewhat similar process of unification the individual must be regarded as subsumed in the universal identifying the Ātman mentioned in this passage with the Supreme Self (*Paramātmā*) or Pure Intelligence (*Cidghana*), according to the Vedāntists.

Much of the interpretation relies, therefore, on this crucial unifying operation—*ekāyanaprakriyā*, as Śaṅkara calls it in his commentary (1.4.19). All possible instances of desire, he says, are subjected to this operation in order to demonstrate that the desire for the Paramātmā is what they have in common. To single out a particular entity as desirable would therefore be to take away from the focus and seriously weaken the argument. Yet single out an individual entity is precisely what Tagore does by choosing the father-son relationship to make his point. Why should he do so? It is a question worth asking because, as a convinced Vedāntist himself, he could have no problem with the thesis that all is comprehended in Brahman. He had propagated this often as a preacher of his own sect of Hindu reformists called the Brahmo, and, more importantly, in his work as a poet, novelist, and essayist. The article under consideration here is replete with the sense of a ubiquitous divine spirit; it abounds in phrases and images that make sense only as a set of Vendāntic notations for the Supreme Self. The distinction between the selves figures prominently in his writings, including one that was addressed to his congregation where he speaks at length on this very upanishadic statement about the parent-child relationship to distinguish between the Small I and the Big I, the Lonely Isolated I and the Comprehensive Great I, My Own I and the Supreme I, and so forth (the phrases used in Bangla being *choto ami, boro ami, eka ami, maha ami, amar ami, param ami,* etc.).[8] All of which makes one wonder why he should have picked one particular desirable out of ten as the basis of his discussion on literature and historicality.

To understand why, one has to keep in mind that this is not the first or only occasion when Tagore uses an upanishadic text entirely in his own way unfettered by textbook Vedāntism. By doing so he has saved this great body of Indian thought from atrophy and archaism, and kept it open as an inexhaustible source of invention for poetry and philosophy. His reading of the extract from the Bṛhadāraṇyaka is itself an instance of that inventiveness. He commented on this at least on six occasions during the last thirty-five years of his life, so far as I can make out, and the readings are all at variance with one another.[9] It is as if there is a torque in the statement that allows the Ātman to be seen in a different light at every turn—sometimes as a paradigm of sovereignty and plenitude, sometimes as a measure of the contrast between the inner and the outer, sometimes as the connectedness of things rather than their isolation, and so forth. Even the authority of Śaṅkara himself had apparently not succeeded in clearing the ambiguity of the original. Enough was left of it to serve as a metaphor on creativity for Tagore when he returned to the text for the last time.

Tagore's reading of that upanishadic saying in his article on literature and historicality has little to do with traditional interpretations based on Śaṅkara's commentaries. "The ātmā," he says in his gloss, "wishes to manifest itself as the creator in its love for its son. That is why it values its love for the son so much." (*Atma putrasneher madhye srishtikartarupe apnake prakash korte cay, tai putrasneha tar kache mulyaban.*) There is nothing here—except for the faintest trace of the most indirect implication—to suggest that these words could be concerned in some sense or other with the relation between a particular set of worldly desires and a general desire (*kāma*) for the Supreme Soul, the problem which the classical Vedāntists and their opponents read in the original passage and were mostly occupied with. Indeed, by isolating the extract from that passage, Tagore severs it from its narrative background in the episode of Maitreyī's dialogue with her husband and frees it from the recursive insistence of the text on the Paramātman's priority over the individual self. Doubly decontextualized in plot and rhetoric, the passage is now ready for a new interpretation with the Ātman understood primarily as a sovereign creative agent—"the Ātmā that needs its love for the son in order to express itself" (*atma jaar nijer prakasher janya putrasneher prayojan*).

The importance of this revision is hard to overestimate. It follows from the logic of a developing critique of historiography. Tagore had already mentioned how essential his childhood experiences were for any understanding of his past as a writer. He did so by citing a number of instances to speak for a facticity he found wanting in the standard histories written about his own work and, by implication, about literature in general. With that done in the first part of the essay, he proceeds to preempt an objection to his argument on the ground that primal experience alone is not enough to refute the claims of those history textbooks. He grants that this could be the case unless the raw material (*upakaran*) of experience, primal or otherwise, were worked creatively into literature. So it is only by confronting historiography with creativity, he suggests, that we can hope to grasp what historicality is about.

As the two sides are lined up, it turns out to be a confrontation between, on the one hand, the externality and publicness of academic historical representation and, on the other, the inwardness of the self's labor of creation and its claim to what accrues inalienably from it. Tagore, championing that claim, has a lot of use here for the upanishadic maxim. For nothing is more completely one's own than what relates parent and child. It is a bond that is paradigmatic for all bonds between progenitor and progeny in every aspect of life including the spheres of artistic and literary work. Here, too, the creator realizes himself in his creation and the latter makes him manifest in his creativity.

It is this unmediated mutuality that constitutes what a writer can claim as his ownmost about self's labor in the creative process. This process had been continuous, for Tagore, with the first stirrings of a sensibility in which he was to find his destiny prefigured as a poet. Which is why the facticity of that self-awakening must be taken into account if his work is to be understood in its essential history. But by the end of his life he had come to believe that such historicality was not, alas, within the competence of academic historiography to tackle.

In the article on literature and historicality, therefore, he attributes that inadequacy to the exclusively public (*sadharon*) stance adopted by historiographical representation. It sees the past only with the public eye and cannot see anything other than what an average seeing would allow. By contrast, everything caught by the creative gaze is seen for the very first time. It is at this point that his recall of those childhood scenes connects with the argument about historicality. And as it happens usually on such occasions when the existential tangles with the epistemological, words tend to slide out of their habitual semantic grooves and are caught up in equivocations that need unraveling.

Itihas, a keyword of this article, exhibits the symptom.[10] Rendered in English as "history," it is used by Tagore to mean both the *historia rerum gestarum* and the *res gestae* themselves. One has to watch, therefore, how he commutes intermittently, yet ever so quickly, between them in speaking of history. Unlike Hegel for whom the collapsing of the two meanings in the same sign, *Geschichte*, was the portent of "a higher order," that is, World-history actualized in writing, Tagore regards it simply as a pretension that masks the poverty of historiography. He insists, therefore, on keeping narrative and event apart as a measure of the distinction between public and creative perception. The light that shone on the coconut fronds, the cumulus suspended high above the house, a cow mothering a foal regardless of distinction in species—none of these had anything to do with the public patterns of historical representation commonly found in academic discourse. Events that speak of a very special relationship between the creator and what he sees, these are not assimilable to historiographical averages. Yet there is no outright rejection of history as he reflects on that past.

> In the *history* of that day there was no one other than myself (*kono dvitiya vyakti*) who saw those clouds in quite the same way (*shei cokkhe*, literally with the same eyes) as I did . . . Rabindranath appeared all alone in that [seeing].

Or,

> In the entire *history* of that day it was Rabindranath alone who witnessed the scene with enchanted eyes. . . . No one else was instructed by the *history* of that day in the profound significance of the sight as was Rabindranath.

I have italicized the word *history* (*itihas*) to indicate how its use in these passages testifies clearly to the historicality of events missed out by the unseeing eye of common historiographical narrative. Far from being the site of a Hegelian "conjunction" between what happens in the past and what is written about it, *itihas* stands here for a line of demarcation between the two. Tagore insists on noticing that line, indeed on highlighting it, not in order to promote the cause of the ahistorical or the unhistorical. On the contrary, it seems to be his intention to demonstrate how history has been impoverished by historiography's preoccupation with the public and the average to the exclusion of the individual and the creative.

According to Tagore the line of demarcation between narrative and event corresponds to what separates the public sphere from the field of creativity (*srishtikshetra*) as well. What was going on in the public sphere with its public "history" was, in his view, merely a statist game of constitutional adjustment—a direct reference, no doubt, to the petty politicking of the time. Even if he could not help being on that side of the line "where history was public" (*itihas jekhane sadharon*) as a matter of necessity, he was there only insofar as he was "a British subject" (he writes that phrase in English), but "not as Rabindranath." Identifying himself by his personal name, he moves to the other side where "in his own field of creativity Rabindranath [was] entirely alone" and "tied to no public by history." There the light that gilded the treetops for him at dawn had little to do with any "statist input owing to the British government" (*British governmenter rashtrik amdani noy*). It was, he writes, rather an effulgence within "some mysterious history of my inner soul (*antaratma*)."

"Mysterious history" and "inner soul": the creative process could hardly be distanced more from public history and the public space of state affairs. Those phrases stand for the utmost inwardness creativity needs to realize itself in literature. It is not enough for it to see things in a new light. For to see is only to collect material that must be worked into literature. "The creator gathers some of the material for his creation from historical narratives and some from his social environment. But the material by itself does not make him a creator. It is only by putting it to use that he expresses himself as the creator."

For collection as well as utilization Tagore relied entirely on his inner self or *antaratma*. It was the latter that constituted his agency (*srishtikartritva*). It gleaned for him not only the fruits of his observation of rural life but also the information gathered from what he had read about early and medieval India. But for all these percepts, physical as well as mental, to be made into literature, such as the lyrics of *Citra*, the stories of *Galpaguccha*, the narrative verses of *Katha O Kahini*, and so forth, he had to be all by himself to get on with the writing. "The creator," he says, "works all alone in his studio (*racanashalay*)."

Solitude had always been an essential condition of creativity for him, and his insistence on it was no exception in this case, as shown by the liberal use of the word *eka* and cognates to mean "lonely," "on one's own," "all by himself," and so forth, throughout the essay. But to construe this to mean withdrawal from history would be entirely wrong. For there is nothing in his long career as a writer to justify such an inference. On the contrary, he made it a point to assert again and again that he belonged to his time and his world. Even when desperately unhappy about the outbreak of the Second World War and "a barbarism terrorizing Europe with its claws and fangs," as he put it in a great essay "Sabhyatar Sankat" (published in English under the title "The Crisis of Civilization"), written only a few months before his death, he was still hoping, although somewhat mystically, that history would come to its own again on a new horizon for humanity. And, as mentioned before, he regarded himself all his life as "a poet of the world." However, what he was unwilling to accept was the reduction of the world to a public space for which alone historiography seemed to have room in its statist narratives. In opposition to that reductive view he argued for a notion of the past big and broad enough to accommodate all of creativity, so that history might fulfill its promise in the plenitude of historicality.

Tagore's critique of historiography in his last statement on the subject is addressed, therefore, to those "pedantic historians" who have narrowed down history in its scope and those literary critics who "wander about so extensively" in history as to rob it of all specificity. "Off with your history!" (*dur hok ge tomar itihas*) is what he would like to say to them. For this so-called history serves no purpose other than to displace the poet from the center of his own creativity. Speaking from that center it is his intention to try and make a case for the marriage of literature and historiography so that the creative insights of one can enrich the other. He cites two instances from his own work to suggest that this can be done. One of these refers to his reading of the standard histories written about precolonial India as part of the curricula of education under the Raj. But "the pictures they formed so clearly in [his] mind," the way he looked at them unlike anyone else before then or since, and the literary works they inspired, owed nothing, he says, to historiography but everything to "Rabindranath's inner soul" alone.

If poetic insight added new dimensions to pasts already interpreted by the history manuals, it probed, in the other instance, the deep structure of historicality in everyday life and represented it in narratives beyond the power of academic historiography to produce. Recalling a very fertile period of his literary career spent in eastern Bengal during the 1890s, he writes:

> There is no doubt that the rural scenes surveyed by the poet's eye in those days were affected by the conflicts of [contemporary] political history (*rashtrik itihaser aghat-pratighat*). However, thanks to his creativity what came to be reflected in *Galpaguccha* [Tagore's book of short stories] was not the image of a feudal order nor of any political order at all, but that history (*itihas*) of the weal and woe of human life which, with its everyday (*pratyahik*) contentment and misery, has always been there in the peasants' fields and village festivals, manifesting their very simple and abiding humanity across all of history—sometimes under Mughal rule, sometimes under British rule.

Here in this passage Tagore finally states in explicit terms what sort of history and historicality he has in mind. He does so first by distinguishing it clearly from the political history of the day. That must have repelled him somewhat as a scene of intrigues and manoeuvres with politicians of all hues haggling over the terms of a constitutional settlement and squabbling about the rival claims of sectarian, sectional and regional interests sponsored by themselves. Tagore concedes that such public affairs could not be left altogether out of history. Yet he is quick to point out that the public (*sadharon*) was constituted in this case by Indians merely as "British subjects" and written up as such in statist historiographies for which he had no respect.

The historicality that he valued himself had another "public" for its protagonist. This was made up of the ordinary men and women who lived in the countryside far away from urban political centers. Since the Swadeshi movement of 1904–1908 rural Bengal had figured in Tagore's thinking, not unlike "Village India" in Gandhi's nearly two decades later, as a metaphor for the greater part of civil society that had not been assimilated to the state. The Mughals, a premodern autocracy, did not covet assimilation. By contrast the British, a modern colonial autocracy, did. However, they failed to achieve it, because it was simply not possible for colonialism, a dominance condemned to rule over the colonized without their consent, hence without hegemony, to persuade its subjects in favor of such a policy. Consequently the life lived in the civil society was never annexed fully to the statist World-history narratives introduced in South Asia by the West. Nor did historiography, its instrument, succeed in penetrating deeply enough the historicality which informed that life. It is precisely this inadequacy that is the object of Tagore's critique.

Literature, he suggests, makes up for historiography's failure in this respect. It does so by addressing the life lived by people in their "everyday contentment and misery." But how can historicality be grasped in terms of the everyday? For an answer one may start by acknowledging what is obvious about the everyday as a peculiar phenomenon in time. Its temporality cannot be identified with any particular day in the calendar that is today or tomorrow, although the characteristic monotony of the everyday is easy to recognize in the current day or the one to come. However, that monotony speaks of the recurrence of something that has been there in all our yesterdays.

Everydayness is thus necessarily informed, like historicality itself, by a sense of the past.

The past which informs everydayness is usually one that is shared, hence public. For, as Heidegger observes, "Everydayness is a way *to be*—to which, of course, that which is publicly manifest belongs."[11] Such a way to be implies being with others in a social time based on a mutually subscribed notion of the past. Without the latter there can be no agreed codes of conduct or rules of comportment to enable people to form anything like a public, nor can there be a tradition or history for such a society to call its own. It is thus that a publicly constituted sense of the past integrates the everyday with the historical and makes it possible for literature to approach historicality along the path of everydayness as claimed by Tagore.

But how can such a claim be sustained solely on the ground of the everyday's pastness and publicness? Wouldn't everydayness as an averaging process level down historicality itself into a dull uniformity? It would, according to Tagore, unless grasped in a creative manner. That is precisely the point he intends to make when he refers to the collection of his short stories, *Galpaguccha*. Its themes are age-old and rendered stale by tradition. But they come alive again by being narrated creatively to show how time and literature work together to recover the living historicality of the quotidian. Tagore relies here on a combination of two of the most commonly used words in his language to explain what he means. To write creatively, he suggests, is to write about *pratyahik sukhduhkha*, that is, about everyday contentment and misery. Now, the Bangla phrase *sukh*, taken by itself, means contentment, happiness, weal, and so on, while *duhkha* stands antonymically for misery, sorrow, woe, and so forth. However, the compound *sukhduhkha* exceeds the sum of their separate meanings to connote, in ordinary usage, something like the entire range of lived experience. When village women meet for a short afternoon break between domestic chores, it is *sukhduhkha* that they talk about. So do people among themselves in the intimate circles of their friends and families, neighbors and colleagues. Thus the discourse of weal and woe, *sukhduhkher katha*, has come to signify the concern that characterizes the solidarities of a shared world. How these solidarities build up and tissues of sharing form in the course of habitual transactions between people, is what *sukhduhkha* is about. By predicating it on the everyday Tagore invests the latter with the concreteness of historicality that he believes to be the privilege and responsibility of creative writing to illuminate and display for unseeing eyes to see.

This stands, of course, for a very different approach to everydayness from that of the scholars described by Henri Lefebvre as "historians of the old school." In his *Critique of Everyday Life* he rebukes them for trivializing everyday life by their obsession with painstaking but irrelevant details and useless descriptions. These amount in his opinion to "whimsical interpretations" and a virtual "sleight of hand" that replaces the concreteness of life by empty abstractions.[12] For contrast, he cites a passage from Marc Bloch's celebrated work on French agrarian history to argue that the familiar deceives by its redundancy, and it requires some insight to grasp the historicality of what lies within the range of everyday perception. "How many times have we all 'strolled' through the French countryside," he writes, "without knowing how to decipher the human landscape before our eyes!" Yet the diversity of field patterns in the same rural scenes yielded to the historian's gaze the long-hidden secrets of the "main types of agrarian civilization" in France. "All we need do is simply to open our eyes," writes Lefebvre. Which is not so different from Tagore's advice. With the poet's reproach about its inadequacy endorsed so vigorously by the philosopher, one had hoped that historiography would pay heed, get rid of its statist blinkers and emulate literature to look afresh at life in order to recuperate the historicality of what is humble and habitual. I am not sure that this has happened in the sixty years since those voices were first heard.

Appendix

Historicality in Literature

Rabindranath Tagore

[The text, "Sahitye Aitihasikata," translated here from the Bangla original, is taken from the centenary edition of Rabindranath Tagore's works, *Rabindra-racanabali* (Kalikata: Paschimbanga Sarkar, Bengali Year 1368), 14:536–38. Dated May 1941, it is chronologically the last article but one of Tagore's prose writings as published in that edition. It is an authorized transcript of what he said in the course of a conversation with Buddhadev Basu, a leader of the younger generation of Bengali writers. Tagore had been engaged in a discussion with them intermittently for some years on questions of modernism and realism in literature. The article has, therefore, a particular poignancy for the history of Bangla literature as a memorial of the last encounter between the foremost representatives of the younger and older generations in the poet's lifetime. He died on 7 August 1941. As discussed in the epilogue, the value of his observations—and strictures—is hard to overestimate for our understanding of historicality.

Tagore was a great essayist. His writings in this genre are exemplary for their lucidity, rigor, and elegance. If these qualities are not always so obvious in this article, it is only because this is *not* an essay but a collection of observations made in the course of a dialogue and in some private correspondence around that time. As such, some of the ellipses and repetitions speak of the spontaneity that is not unusual in such exchanges. We have done nothing, in this translation, to alter or amend these stylistic peculiarities of the article. Nor have we taken the liberty to break up the long second paragraph, for we suspect that it stands perhaps for an uninterrupted stretch and the editors of the original text intended to let it stay that way.

The translation is mine. I have added a few notes on some of the bibliographical and biographical details mentioned in the article.—Trans.]

I have heard it said again and again that we are guided altogether by history, and I have energetically nodded, so to say, in my mind whenever I heard it. I have settled this debate in my own heart where I am nothing but a poet. I am there in the role of a creator all alone and free. There's little to enmesh me there in the net of external events. I find it difficult to put up with the pedantic historian when he tries to force me out of the center of my creativity as a poet. Let us go back to the inaugural moment of my poetical career.

It's a daybreak in winter. A pale light is beginning to filter through the darkness. We were like the poor in our ways. There was no extravagance about our use of winter garments. One just slipped into a top of some kind on leaving the warmth of the duvet. But there was really no need to rush. Like everyone else I, too, could have stayed happily curled up in bed until at least six in the morning. But it was not possible for me to do so. There was a garden within the inner precincts of our house. Indigent like myself, all it had for its wealth was mostly a row of coconut trees lining the eastern wall. Yet I used to be in such a hurry lest I should miss anything of what I saw every day as the light fell on the trembling coconut fronds and the dewdrops burst into glitter. I used to think that this joy of the welcoming dawn would be of interest to all the other boys as well. If that were true, it would have been easy to explain it in terms of the universality of child behavior. No other explanation would have been necessary had it been known that I was not set apart from the others by the very force of this excessive curiosity of mine and that I was just as ordinary. But as I grew older I came to realize that there was no other child nearly so keen to see the light vibrating on shrubs and trees. I found out, too, that none of those who had grown up with me fitted into this particular category of madness. Not to speak of them alone, there was nobody in my entire milieu who felt deprived that he hadn't been out, dressed warmly or not, to see the play of light even once. There's nothing in it that comes out of the mold of history. Had that been the case a crowd would have turned up in that miserable garden at dawn with everyone competing to be the first to see and grasp that entire scene by heart. It is precisely in this that one is a poet. One day I had just come back from school at about four-thirty and found a dark blue cumulus suspended high above the third storey of our house. What a marvelous sight that was. Even now I remember that day. But in the history of that day there was no one other than myself who saw those clouds in quite the same way as I did or was similarly thrilled. Rabindranath happened to be all by himself in that instance. Once after school I saw a most amazing spectacle from our western verandah. A donkey—not one of those donkeys manufactured by British imperial policy but the animal that had always belonged to our own society and has not changed in its ways since the beginning of time—one such donkey had come up from the washermen's quarters and was grazing on the grass while a cow fondly licked its body. The attraction of one living being for another that then caught my eye has remained unforgettable for me until today. In the entire history of that day it was Rabindranath alone who witnessed the scene with enchanted eyes. This I know for certain. No one else was instructed by the history of that day in the profound significance of the sight as was Rabindranath. In his own field of creativity Rabindranath has been entirely alone and tied to no public by history. Where history was public, he was there merely as a British subject but not as Rabindranath himself. The bizarre game of political change was being played out there, of course, but the light that glittered on the foliage of coconut palms was not a statist input owing to the British government. It radiated within some mysterious history of my inner soul and manifested itself in its own blissful form every day in various ways. As it has been said in our Upanishads: "It is not for the sake of the sons, my dear, that they are loved, but for one's own sake that they are loved." The *ātmā* wishes to manifest itself as the creator in its love for its son. That is why it values its love for the son so much. The creator gathers some of the material for his creation from historical narratives and some from his social environment. But the material by itself does not make him a creator. It is only by putting it to use that he expresses himself as the creator. There are many events that are there waiting to be known, and it is only by chance that we get to know them. There was a time when I had come to be acquainted with the Buddhist and other historical accounts, and these assumed a pictorial clarity to inspire me with a creative urge. All of a sudden the narratives of *Katha O Kahini* surged like a headspring and branched off in several directions.[1] One could possibly have come to learn about these histories as part of one's education those days. *Katha O Kahini* could therefore be said to be a work that belonged to its time. But it is not because of history that Rabindranath was the only one to be so blissfully moved as he was by the form and aesthetic content of *Katha O Kahini*. The reason lies in his inner soul. Which is why it has been said that the self alone is the agent. To push that in the background and flaunt the raw material of history may be a matter of pride for some. They may even rob the agent of a part of his creative joy for their own benefit. But all this is secondary, as the creator knows. The monk Upagupta emerges from the entire set-up of the history of Buddhism to present himself to Rabindranath alone, and in what glory, what compassion does he do so![2] Had it been an authentic exercise in historiography, *Katha O Kahini* would have been celebrated throughout the land. No other person had looked at these pictures in the same way until then or since. Indeed, it is precisely because of the distinctive character of the poet's creativity that people have come to enjoy it. Once when I used to travel by boat along the rivers of Bengal and came to sense its playful vitality, my inner soul delighted in gathering those wonderful impressions of weal and woe in my heart which were composed into sketches of country life month after month in a way nobody had done before.[3] For the creator works all alone in his studio. Like the Supreme Creator, he, too, creates his work out of his own self. There is no doubt that the rural scenes surveyed by the poet in those days were affected by the conflicts of political history. However, thanks to his creativity, what came to be reflected in *Galpaguccha*[4] was not the image of a feudal order nor indeed any political order at all, but that history of the weal and woe of human life which, with its everyday contentment and misery, has always been there in the peasants' fields and village festivals, manifesting their simple and abiding humanity across all of history—sometimes under Mughal rule, sometimes under British rule. I am not acquainted with at least three-quarters of that far-flung history in which the critics of today wander about so extensively. That is why I guess it upsets me so much. I have it in my mind to say, "Off with your history." At the helm of my own vessel of creativity I have the *ātmā* that needs its love for the son in order to express itself. It assimilates to its work the multifarious spectacles of the world with all its happiness and sadness. It takes delight in doing so and sharing its joy with others. I have not been able to put the entire history of my life in words, but that history is of no importance. It is the desire for self-expression on the part of man as the creator that has engaged him in all his long endeavor over the ages. Try and highlight only the history which is piloted by man-as-creator towards the Magnum that lies beyond history and is at the very center of the human soul. This was known to our Upanishads. The message the Upanishads have for me is what I have taken from them on my own initiative. That stands for an agenthood which is mine alone.

Santiniketan, May 1941

Notes

1. Introduction

1. Karl Marx, "Economic and Philosophical Manuscripts of 1844," in Karl Marx and Friedrich Engels, *Collected Works* (London: Lawrence and Wishart, 1975), 3:340.
2. Ibid., pp. 340–41, and p. 605 n. 105.
3. Georg Wilhelm Friedrich Hegel, *Lectures on the Philosophy of World History. Introduction*, trans. H. B. Nisbet (Cambridge: Cambridge University Press, 1975), p. 42.
4. Ibid., pp. 67, 93, 94.
5. *Plutarch's Lives* (London: J. M. Dent, 1939), 2:473.
6. Hegel, *Lectures on the Philosophy of World History*, p. 141.
7. Ibid.

2. Historicality and the Prose of the World

1. Aristotle, *Metaphysics: Books Γ, Δ, E*, trans. Christopher Kirwan (Oxford: Clarendon, 1971), Δ17, p. 54.
2. Ludwig Wittgenstein, *Tractacus Logico-Philosophicus* (London: Routledge, 1989), p. 3.
3. Walter D. Mignolo, *The Darker Side of the Renaissance* (Ann Arbor: University of Michigan Press, 1995), p. 127.
4. G.W.F. Hegel, *Lectures on the Philosophy of World History. Introduction: Reason in History*, trans. H. B. Nisbet (Cambridge: Cambridge University Press, 1982), pp. 164, 165. Hereafter, *Lectures on World History*.

5. Ibid., p. 136 (emphasis added).
6. The most authoritative modern version of this work, published in 1801 at the Baptist Mission Press (Serampore), is Ramram Basu, *Raja Pratapaditya Caritra*, edited and introduced by Brajendranath Bandyopadhyay (Kalikata: Ranjan Publishing House, Bengali Year 1343). Reprinted in the Dushprapya Granthamala or Rare Books series of Ranjan Publishing House, it is now a rare book itself. It is entirely owing to Professor Gautam Bhadra's kindness that I have been able to acquire a copy of this valuable text for my use.
7. Carey to Ryland (15 June 1801). Cited in Brajendranath Bandyopadhyay, *Ramram Basu* (Kalikata: Bangiya-sahitya-parishat, 1941), p. 27.
8. Carey to Rothman (n.d.), in ibid., p. 29.
9. Ramram Basu, *Raja Pratapaditya Caritra*, p. 1.
10. For a brilliant study of the distinction between the modern historical narrative and the premodern chronicle, see Hayden White, *The Content of the Form* (Baltimore: The Johns Hopkins University Press, 1987), chap. 1, esp. p. 17.
11. Carey to Ryland (15 June 1801), in Bandyopadhyay, *Ramram Basu*, p. 27 (emphasis added).
12. Paolo Rossi, *The Dark Abyss of Time* (Chicago: University of Chicago Press, 1987), p. 171.
13. Etienne Bonnot de Condillac, *An Essay on the Origin of the Human Language* (Gainsville, Fla.: Scholars' Facsimiles & Reprints, 1971), pp. 227–29.
14. Ibid., p. 299.
15. Jacques Derrida, *The Archeology of the Frivolous: Reading Condillac* (Pittsburgh: Duquesne University Press, 1980), p. 67.
16. Ibid., p. 64.
17. Condillac, *Essay*, p. 299.
18. G.W.F. Hegel, *Phenomenology of Spirit*, trans. A. V. Miller. (Oxford: Clarendon, 1977), p. 492.
19. Ibid., p.488.
20. G.W.F. Hegel, *Aesthetics* (Oxford: Clarendon, 1975), 2:973.
21. Hegel, *Lectures on World History*, p. 136.
22. Bandyopadhyay, *Ramram Basu*, p. 8.
23. Ward's journal (25 May 1800), cited in ibid., p. 11.
24. Hegel, *Phenomenology*, pp. 178–79.
25. G.W.F. Hegel, *Logic*, trans. William Wallace (Oxford: Clarendon, 1978), pp. 239–40.
26. Jean Hyppolite, *Genesis and Structure of Hegel's Phenomenology of Spirit* (Evanston: Northwestern University Press, 1974), p. 323.
27. Hegel, *Phenomenology*, p. 110.
28. Ibid., p. 111.
29. Ibid., p. 112.

30. Hegel, *Aesthetics*, 1:149.
31. Ibid., p. 150.
32. Ibid., pp. 268, 597, 598 (emphasis added).
33. Hegel, *Phenomenology*, p. 105.
34. Hyppolite, *Genesis and Structure*, p. 160.
35. Jacques Lacan, *Écrits: A Selection* (London: Tavistock, 1980), p. 167.
36. Hegel, *Aesthetics*, 1:150.
37. Hegel, *Aesthetics*, 2:988.
38. Ibid., p. 989.

3. *The Prose of History, or The Invention of World-History*

1. Hegel, *Lectures on World History*, p. 128.
2. G.W.F. Hegel, *Elements of the Philosophy of Right*, ed. Allen W. Wood (Cambridge: Cambridge University Press, 1991), no. 342, p. 372 (emphasis added). Hereafter, *Philosophy of Right*.
3. Hegel, *Lectures on World History*, pp. 46, 126.
4. Hegel, *Philosophy of Right*, no. 258, p. 279.
5. G.W.F. Hegel, *Logic*, trans. William Wallace (Oxford: Clarendon, 1978), no. 142, p. 201.
6. Hegel, *Lectures on World History*, p. 131.
7. Ibid., p. 64.
8. Ibid. (emphasis added).
9. Hegel, *Logic*, no. 142, pp. 200–201.
10. Hegel, *Lectures on World History*, p. 46.
11. Antoine-Nicolas de Condorcet, *Sketch for a Historical Picture of the Progress of the Human Mind*, trans. J. Barraclough (London: Weidenfeld and Nicholson, 1955).
12. Charles Taylor, *Hegel* (Cambridge: Cambridge University Press, 1975), p. 74, and pp. 72–75, passim.
13. Hegel, *Logic*, no. 145, p. 206.
14. Hegel, *Lectures on World History*, pp. 28, 35.
15. Hegel, *Lectures on World History*, p. 127.
16. Ibid., p. 125.
17. Swami Vireswarananda, *Brahmasūtras* (Calcutta: Advaita Ashrama, 1936; reprint 1982), p. 8. There is also a Sāṃkhya version of *adhyāsa*, as Surendranath Dasgupta points out in *A History of Indian Philosophy*, 1:493.
18. Hegel, *Lectures on World History*, p. 55.
19. Ibid., p. 128.
20. Ibid., pp. 128–29.
21. Ibid., p. 124.

22. Ibid., p. 128.
23. Ibid., pp. 128–29.
24. Ibid., p. 128.
25. Ibid., pp. 126–27.
26. Ibid., p. 131.
27. Ibid., p. 12 (emphasis added).
28. Hegel, *Philosophy of Right*, no. 352, p. 376.
29. Hegel, *Philosophy of Right*, no. 355, p. 378 (emphasis added).
30. Hegel, *Lectures on World History*, p. 130.
31. Ibid.
32. Ibid., p. 131.
33. Ibid., p. 140.
34. Ibid., p. 144.
35. Ibid., p. 145.
36. Hegel, *Aesthetics*, 2:1094.
37. Ibid., p. 1073.
38. Ibid., p. 1095.
39. Hegel, *Lectures on World History*, p. 134.
40. Ibid., p. 120.
41. Ibid., p. 97.
42. Ibid., p. 94.
43. Hegel, *Philosophy of Right*, no. 258; addition, p. 279. Charles Taylor (*Hegel*, p. 367 and n. 1) follows W. Kaufmann to remind us that the original, "Es ist der Gang Gottes in der Welt, daß der Staat ist," mistranslated as "The state is the march of God through the world," made Hegel subject to allegations about sympathy for Prussianism.
44. Jean Hyppolite, *Studies on Marx and Hegel* (London: Heinemann, 1969), p. 108.
45. Ernst Cassirer, *The Myth of the State* (New Haven: Yale University Press, 1946; reprint 1974), pp. 272, 273.
46. For this information on the ethnic constituents of Hegel's "Germanic Realm" I have relied on the editorial note in *Philosophy of Right*, pp. 479–80.
47. Hegel, *Lectures on World History*, pp. 54, 131.
48. Hegel, *Philosophy of Right*, no. 350, p. 376.
49. Hegel, *Aesthetics*, 1:185–86.
50. Hegel, *Philosophy of Right*, no. 351, p. 376 (emphasis added).
51. See Ranajit Guha, *A Rule of Property for Bengal: An Essay on the Idea of Permanent Settlement* (Durham, N.C.: Duke University Press, 1996), p. 155.
52. Hegel, *Philosophy of Right*, no. 327, pp. 364, 474 n.
53. Hegel, *Aesthetics*, 2:1061–62 (emphasis added).

54. For a detailed discussion on these aspects of the Raj, see Ranajit Guha, *Dominance Without Hegemony* (Cambridge, Mass.: Harvard University Press, 1997), chap. 3 and passim.
55. Hayden White, *Metahistory* (Baltimore: The Johns Hopkins University Press, 1983), p. 85.

4. Experience, Wonder, and the Pathos of Historicality

1. Aristotle, *Posterior Analytics*, trans. Jonathan Barnes (Oxford: Clarendon, 1975), p. 1.
2. Ibid., B 19, pp. 80–82, 248–60 nn.
3. White, *Metahistory*, p. 5.
4. Daniel H. H. Ingalls, ed., *The Dhvanyāloka of Ānandavardhana with the Locana of Abhinavagupta* (Cambridge, Mass.: Harvard University Press, 1990), pp. 52–53 n. 2.
5. See "An Indian Historiography of India: Hegemonic Implications of a Nineteenth-Century Agenda," in Guha, *Dominance Without Hegemony*, chap. 3, pp. 156–76 and passim.
6. The closest Bidyalankar approaches *itihāsa* is by compounding it with *purāṇa*. The term *purāṇetihāsa* thus obtained refers to the genre of traditional, mostly mythic, narratives of which the Rāmāyaṇa and the Mahābhārata are the best-known exemplars. The word *upākhyāna*, too, occurs a couple of times in *Rajabali*, but it is *vivaraṇa* that the author uses generally for "narrative" throughout his work.
7. Ram Comul Sen, *A Dictionary in English and Bengalee Translated from Todd's Edition of Johnson's English Dictionary* (Serampore: Serampore Press, 1834). Ram Comul Sen was Native Secretary to the Asiatick, and Agricultural and Horticultural Societies, etc.
8. Hegel, *Lectures on World History*, p. 135.
9. Ian Watt, *The Rise of the Novel* (Harmondsworth: Penguin, 1970), p. 33.
10. Ibid., p. 15.
11. M. M. Bakhtin, *The Dialogic Imagination* (Austin: University of Texas Press, 1981), pp. 15, 39.
12. White, *Metahistory*, p. 8 n. 6.
13. Hegel, *Lectures on World History*, p. 12.
14. Watt, *The Rise of the Novel*, p. 35 and n. 1.
15. On the changing reputation of Herodotus as a historian, see François Hartog, *The Mirror of Herodotus* (Berkeley: University of California Press, 1988), chap. 7, conclusion.
16. Edward Said, *Beginnings* (New York: Columbia University Press, 1988), pp. 81–82.

17. See Guha, *Dominance Without Hegemony*, pp. 176–88, for an elaborate discussion of this question.
18. *Mahābhārata*, 1.1.6–7. All references are to the standard BORI edition; hereafter, *MBh*.
19. See n. 4, above.
20. See *āścaryamanitye* (6.1.147) and *vṛtti* in the *Aṣṭādhyāyī*.
21. Sushil Kumar De, *History of Sanskrit Poetics*, 2nd rev. ed. (Calcutta: Firma K. L. Mukhopadhyay, 1960), 2:135.
22. Hans-Georg Gadamer, *Truth and Method* (New York: Crossroad, 1988), p. 60.
23. Stephen Greenblatt, *Marvelous Possessions* (Chicago: University of Chicago Press, 1991), p. 20.
24. Martin Heidegger, *Being and Time*, trans. J. Stambaugh (Albany: State University of New York Press, 1966), p. 161.
25. *Aristotle's Metaphysics*, trans. Christopher Kirwan (Oxford: Clarendon, 1971).
26. Walter Benjamin, "The Storyteller," in *Illuminations* (London: Fontana, 1973), p. 90.
27. Martin Heidegger, *Basic Questions of Philosophy* (Bloomington: Indiana University Press, 1994), p. 140.
28. The summary of Abhinavagupta's views that follows is based on his *Locana* on Ānandavardhana's *Dhvanyāloka*, 1.5, 1.18, and passim.
29. Ramiero Gnoli, *The Aesthetic Experience According to Abhinavagupta* (Varanasi: Chowkhamba, 1968), p. xlvii.
30. Ibid., pp. 33–41, 88–101.
31. The text, Abhinavagupta's *Abhinavabhāratī*, reads: *mukhyāmukhyāvalokane ca tadanukaraṇapratibhāsaḥ* (ibid., p. 6).
32. Bakhtin, *The Dialogic Imagination*, p. 38.
33. Ibid., p. 13. See the translator's note on Bakhtin's modification of the phrase used by Goethe and Schiller.
34. Lukács, *The Theory of the Novel* (London: Merlin, 1971), p. 122.
35. Bakhtin, *The Dialogic Imagination*, p. 13.
36. Ibid., pp. 15–16.
37. Hegel, *Lectures on the Philosophy of World History*, p. 127.
38. Ibid., p. 32.
39. Hegel, *Aesthetics*, 2:907.
40. Hegel, *Aesthetics*, 1:459.
41. Hegel, *Lectures on World History*, pp. 145, 147.
42. Ibid., p. 136.
43. Ibid., p. 12.
44. Rabindranath Thakur, *Rabindra-racanabali*, centenary edition (Kalikata: Paschimbanga Sarkar, Bengali Year 1368), 14:536–38.

45. Northrop Frye, *Anatomy of Criticism* (London: Penguin, 1990), pp. 38–39.
46. Ibid., p. 39. The reference is apparently to "The Sailor's Mother" (1802; published 1807).

5. *Epilogue: The Poverty of Historiography—A Poet's Reproach*

1. All citations in Bangla from this article refer to "Sahitye Aitihasikata," in *Rabindra-racanabali*, 14:536–38.
2. Immanuel Kant, *Critique of Pure Reason*, trans. Norman Kemp Smith (London: Macmillan, 1990), p. 505.
3. Martin Heidegger, *Being and Time*, trans. Joan Stambaugh (Albany: State University of New York Press, 1996), p. 52.
4. "Janmadine," no. 10, in *Rabindra-racanabali*, 3:845.
5. *Rabindra-racanabali*, 10:11.
6. Surendranath Dasgupta, A *History of Indian Philosophy* (Delhi: Motilal Banarsidass, 1997), 1:14, 33.
7. Translations of this text and Śankarācārya's commentary on it are all taken from *The Bṛhadāraṇyaka Upaniṣad*, trans. Swami Madhavananda (Calcutta: Advaita Ashrama, 1988). This conversation between Yājñavalkya and Maitreyī occurs twice in the Bṛhadāraṇyaka—in 2.4.5 and again, with minor variations, in 4.5.6. We have used the first of these two passages.
8. "Bairagya," in *Satiniketan*, pp. 215–17: *Rabindra-racanabali* 12.
9. The articles, dated according to the Bengali calendar, are "Viswasahitya" (1313) in *Rabindra-racanabali*, vol. 13; "Bairagya" (1315), ibid., vol. 12; "Manusher Dharma" (1349), ibid., vol. 12; "Sahityatattva" (1340), ibid., vol. 14; "Utsarga" (1343), in *Sahityer Pathe*, ibid.; "Sahitye Aitihasikata" (1348), ibid.
10. For a detailed discussion of *itihāsa*, the Sanskrit term from which the vernacular *itihas* is derived, see chapter 4 in this volume.
11. Martin Heidegger, *Being and Time*, trans. John Macquarrie and Edward Robinson. (Oxford: Basil Blackwell, 1987), p. 422.
12. Henri Lefebvre, *Critique of Everyday Life, Volume I: Introduction*, trans. John Moore (London: Verso, 1992). Citations from this work are all from chapter 2: "The Knowledge of Everyday Life," pp. 130–37. The original, *Critique de la vie quotidienne I: Introduction*, was published first by Grasset, Paris, 1947.

Appendix: Historicality in Literature by Rabindranath Tagore

1. *Katha O Kahini*, mentioned thrice in this article, is a collection of Tagore's narrative poems. In a prefatory note he identifies the contents of *Katha*, the

larger part of the collection, as what is "called narrative in the poetics of English literature" (*Rabindra-racanabali* 1:608). The note anticipates in several respects his recall of the work forty years later in "Sahitye Aitihasikata." The production of the work, in two short bursts of intense creativity in 1897 and 1899, is described in the same gushing imageries of tidal waves and inundations. The pictorial view of the narrative, too, is already there. "Considered carefully," he writes, "the poems of *Katha*, although classified as narratives, make up a gallery of pictures. . . . Each stands for a discrete visual scene." Not the least relevant for our discussion, he mentions how it was precisely because of such visuality and its "externalizing tendency" (*chhabir abhimukhita bairer dike*) that he had landed in "the realm of history" (*itihaser rajye*) looking for material.

2. Tagore drew on Indian myths and histories for the narrative poems of *Katha* (see n. 1, above). As many as eight out of the twenty-four narratives that make up the text were based on his readings of the literature on Buddhism. The very fine poem, "Abhisar" (*Rabindra-racanabali* 1:626–28) is based on the episode "Upagupta Avadana" of the *Bodhisattvāvadāna-kalpalatā*, in which the young monk Upagupta returns a courtesan's lust by compassion. Retold by Tagore the story is considerably modified, as one would expect. On this and other adaptations from Buddhist literature by Tagore for his narratives in *Katha*, see Prasantakumar Pal, *Rabijibani* 4:250–51.
3. This refers to a period of nearly eleven years from the end of 1889 spent by Tagore in a part of eastern Bengal. He was there to look after the large estates owned by his family and spent a great deal of his time moving by boat from village to village in those riverine districts. It turned out to be the most productive and, according to some, the most creative decade of his literary career.
4. *Galpaguccha* is Tagore's book of short stories, the first volume of which was published in 1900.

Glossary

aitihya	tradition.
ākhyāna	narrative, story.
ārambhaka	lit., initiator; one who initiates a musical, theatrical, or storytelling session by requesting the performers to begin their act.
ātman, ātmā	self, soul, spirit.
avyaya	a linguistic entity that is not subject to rules of declension according to Sanskrit grammar.
Bangla	the language of the Bengali people who make up the greater part of the populations of Bangladesh and the West Bengal state of India.
Dalit	lit., the oppressed; a term used in contemporary India to refer to the most discriminated sections of the population within the Hindu caste hierarchy.
dhvani	the theory of suggestion formulated and propagated by an influential school of Indian poetics under Ānandavardhana and Abhinavagupta.
Diwani	the office of Diwan under the Nawab of Bengal, Bihar, and Orissa. In 1765, eight years after the conquest of Bengal, the English East India Company acquired this office by an arrangement with the Nawab. The control of land revenues and the administration of judicial matters concerned with landed property passed thereafter into the Company's hands.
itihāsa	the genre of ancient Indian narrative that has the past for its object. The Sanskrit term has been adapted by a number of South Asian vernaculars as *itihas* to mean history and historiography in a modernist sense.

jāti	genus.
kathā	tale, story.
Mahābhārata	the name of one of the two great Indian epic narratives, the other being the Rāmāyaṇa (q.v.).
māyāvāda	the doctrine of illusion, which is central to the interpretation of Advaita Vedānta philosophy according to Śaṅkara.
pāraṃparya	succession, sequentiality.
purāṇa	generic name for a body of mythic accounts composed in Sanskrit verse.
purāṇetihāsa	a compound of *purāṇa* (q.v.) and *itihāsa* (q.v.), meaning ancient narratives of which the most famous exemplars are the Mahābhārata (q.v.) and the Rāmāyaṇa (q.v.).
Rāmāyaṇa	one of the two great Indian epic narratives, the other being the Mahābhārata (q.v.).
rasa	flavor, relish, juice, extract. In Indian poetics it constitutes the very essence of aesthetic, as opposed to emotional response, according to Abhinavagupta.
Sāṃkhya	one of the principal schools of ancient Indian philosophy.
upākhyāna	a tale or episode that constitutes some part or subdivision of a larger narrative like *ākhyāna* (q.v.).
Upaniṣad	a collection of ancient metaphysical treatises, the earliest of which goes back to circa 700 B.C. Distinguished from other kinds of post-Vedic literature by its emphasis on epistemology, the Upaniṣad consists of at least 112 separate treatises according to Surendranath Dasgupta. The corpus, taken as a whole, is often anglicized as the Upanishads.
Vedānta	the most influential school of Indian monistic philosophy. It is not known for certain when exactly its foundational theses, the *Brahmasūtras*, were first enunciated. However, it is generally agreed that Vedānta owes its preeminence to its interpretation by Śaṅkara (788–820 A.D.) and especially to his commentary on those theses.
viparyāsakaraṇa	the operation of shifting in Sanskrit semantics, especially as it occurs in "the shifting of a meaning from the object to the word for the object," according to Daniel Ingalls.
vyakti	individual.

Index

Abhinavagupta, 62, 110, 106n28, 106n31; and the Dhvani school of poetics, 109; on *rasa* of wonder, 66–68 passim
adbhuta, 62, 66–67; as *rasa* of wonder, 62–63, 66; and *thaumazein*, 65–66
Aesthetics (Hegel), 18, 24, 41, 46
ākhyāna, 109, 110; as *archai*, 50; and *itihāsa*, 161
Amarakośa, 59; on *itihāsa*, 50–51, 60; on wonder, 62
Ānandavardhana, 62, 106n28, 109
annal, 11, 15
ārambhaka, 109; grammarians on, 58–59; role of, 59
Aristotle: on the concept of *archai*, 49–50; limit defined by, 7; *Posterior Analytics*, 49; on truth, 64
āścarya, 62, 106n20

Bakhtin, Michael: on epic past, 69; on primacy of experience, 55
Bangla, 10, 11, 12, 85, 93, 95, 109
Bankimchandra Chattopadhyay, 76
Basu. *See* Ramram Basu
Benjamin, Walter: and a reading of Herodotus, 65–66; on wonder in historical narrative, 65
Bloch, Marc, 94
The Bṛhadāraṇyaka, 82–84, 107n7; Śaṅkara on, 84–85; Tagore's reading of, 82, 85–86
Buddhadev Basu, 76, 95

Carey, William, 52; and Indian historiography, 72; and Ramram Basu, 10–12
Cassirer, Ernst, 40
chronicle: Persian, 11; precolonial, 15, 102n10; White on, 50
Clive, Robert, 10, 42
Columbus, Christopher, 9, 12, 43
Condillac, Etienne Bonnot de: Derrida on, 13; *An Essay on the Origin of the Human Language*, 13–14; secular view of language, 13
Condorcet, Antoine-Nicolas de, 24; and man-centered view of progress,

Condorcet (*continued*)
28; his *Sketch for a Historical Picture of the Progress of the Human Mind*, 28
curiosity, 11, 14, 46, 58, 96; and *adbhutarasa*, 66; Heidegger on, 65; *see also* wonder

Dasgupta. *See* Surendranath Dasgupta
De. *See* Sushil Kumar De
Defoe, Daniel, 55, 64
Derrida, Jacques, 7, 13
Dhṛtarāṣṭra, 58, 60

East India Company, 12, 42, 51, 52, 109–10; and Fort William College, 10, 52; and the uses of Prehistory, 44; and World-history, 51
Elements of the Philosophy of Right (Hegel), 2, 3, 25, 36, 41, 42
The Encyclopaedia (Hegel), 3, 25
Enlightenment, 12; and Hegel, 2, 27; and universal history, 28
epic, 110; and the absolute past, 69; Bakhtin on, 55, 69; Indian, Hegel on 38, 40; narrative in the Mahābhārata, 56–62; novelization of, 55; as *purāṇetihāsa*, 52–53; and Western superiority, 43
everyday, 49; and desire, 20–21; Heidegger on, 93; historicality of, 91–94; history as narrative of, 6, 75; and inadequacy of historiography, 73, 92, 94; Lefebvre on historicality of, 94; as the present, 20, 21; and prose of the world, 18–21; and striving for recognition, 21–22; Tagore on, 91–94 passim, 99; and temporal particularity, 7, 21; and wonder, 68
experience, 6, 16, 21, 50, 74–80 passim, 87, 93; Bakhtin on, 55, 69; centrality and immediacy of, 55, 60, 61, 63–64, 66; Gadamer on, 63–64; Greenblatt on, 64; Hegel on, 55; and historiography, 55, 69, 71–72; and Indian tradition, 60–61, 66–68; narrative of, 48, 63–64, 69; and the novel, 48, 55, 56, 69, 71; and repetition, 61–62; and time, 69–72 passim; and truth, 63–64; Watt on, 55; wonder vanquished by, 72

Frye, Northrop: on pathos, 73–74

Gadamer, Hans-Georg: on immediacy of experience, 63–64
Geist, 14, 32, 42, 48; concept of, 3; and man, 28; plan of, 29, 30; and self-consciousness, 35; and World-history, 27; *see also* God; Spirit
Geschichte, ambiguity of, 53, 88
Gnoli, Raniero, on the aesthetics of wonder, 66–67
God, 14, 46, 82; concept of, 3; design of, 29; Hegel on, 3–4; and state, 39, 104n43; and World-history, 28–29
Greenblatt, Stephen: on experience and wonder, 64

Hegel, G. W. F., 2, 3, 7, 9, 10, 15–45 passim, 48, 53–54; and *Aufhebung*, 2–3; and China, 32, 37–38, 41; on the East and the Eastern, 38, 43; on *Geist*, 28, 29, 32, 35, 42; on God, 3, 4, 28–29, 39, 46; on Herodotus, 55, 71; on India, 7, 9, 10, 32, 37, 38, 40, 52; on memory, 70–72; on the Orient and the Oriental,

35–37, 40; on prose and poetry, 14–24 passim, 38; on prose of history, 15, 16, 24–47 passim; on prose of the world, 7–23 passim; on stages of history, 27, 32–34; on Thucydides, 55, 71; on time and history, 70–72; on World-historical realms, 35–38, 40; *see also* state
Heidegger, Martin: on curiosity as distinct from wonder, 65; on everydayness and being, 93; on factuality and facticity, 79; on *thaumazein*, 65–66
Herodotus, 64; Benjamin's reading of, 65–66; and immediacy of experience, 55, 71; as "father of all liars," 55
historiography, 8, 24, 44, 52, 53, 110; and its *archai*, 50; and colonialism, 44–45, 48–49; and everyday life, 73; and experience, 55, 69; as act of expropriation, 1–2; and God, 29; and Hegel, 29–31, 46, 71; and historicality, 5, 7, 22, 45, 46, 54; inadequacy and poverty of, 5, 6, 72, 75–99 passim; and Prehistory, 44–45; and Ramram Basu's work, 10–12, 15–16; South Asian, 1, 5, 49, 73; statism in, 5, 10, 40, 46, 71, 73; and World-history, 24, 44, 49, 54, 56, 74; *see also* Rabindranath Tagore
Hyppolite, Jean: on desire and intersubjectivity in self-consciousness, 21; on Hegel's politics, 39

Ingalls, Daniel, 50–51, 60
itihāsa, 48, 110; etymology of, 50–51, 60–61, 68; and experience, 60–61, 67; the Mahābhārata as, 56; as narrative of wonder, 68; translated into history, 48, 52–53; and World-history, 51, 54, 62, 72

Jadunath Sarkar, 11
Janamejaya, 58

Kaiyaṭa, 58, 60, 61
Kant, Immanuel, 9, 64, 79; on the real and the possible, 78
kathā, 57, 110; as *archai*, 50; initiated by listeners, 56; as tales of wonder, 62
kathāyoga, 58

Lacan, Jacques, on metonymy of desire, 21
Lectures on the Philosophy of World History (Hegel), 3, 9, 25, 28, 29, 34, 35, 36, 46, 71
Lefebvre, Henri, *Critique of Everyday Life*, 94; *see also* everyday
limit, 48, 74; Aristotle on, 7; concept of, 7–8; of language, 6; statehood as, 10; Wittgenstein on, 8, 16; of World-history, 4, 6, 7, 16, 24, 47
Logic (Hegel), 29
Lukács, Georg, 56, 69

The Mahābhārata, 110, 105n6; Hegel on, 38; as *itihāsa*, 51, 52; the listener in, 56, 61–62; storytelling in, 56–62
Maitreyī, 82, 83, 84, 86; Yājñavalkya's address to, 83–84
Marx, Karl: on *Aufhebung*, 2–3; on Hegel's *Elements of the Philosophy of Right*, 2–3; on Hegel's politics, 39
memory, 50, 66, 70, 71; *see also* Hegel
Mignolo, Walter, on people without history, 8

Mill, James, 1
Mnemosyne, Hegel on, 70, 71, 72
Montaigne, 65
Mrityunjoy Bidyalankar, 52, 105n6

Nāgeśa, 59, 61
narration, 57, 62, 67
narrative, 22, 47, 52, 64; *ākhyāna* genre of, 109, 110; of being-with-others, 73; Benjamin on, 65–66; cycle, 58, 59; and event, 30, 31, 53, 88–89; of experience, 48, 55–56, 63–70 passim; historical, 11, 13, 31, 45, 49, 53, 75, 89, 91, 102n10; Indian epics as, 105n6, 110; *itihāsa* as, 51, 67, 68, 110; in Mrityunjoy Bidyalankar's work, 105n6; competing paradigms of, 54, 63; of prose of history, 54; of public affairs, 5; and Ramram Basu's work, 10–12 passim; of Spirit's development, 31, 34; statist, 72, 90; and Tagore, 75, 86, 89, 98, 107n1, 108n2; of wonder, 48, 62, 68
narratology: Indian, 62; revolutionized by colonialist knowledge, 5–6; of World-history, 47
narrator: and authority of beginning, 55; in autobiography, 64; and the listeners' initiative, 59, 72; in the Mahābhārata, 57–59, 61; in the Rāmāyaṇa, 66
Nikhilnath Ray, 11
novel, 48, 60, 75; and authenticity, 55, 63; Bakhtin on, 55, 69; and experience, 48, 55–56; and history, 56, 69; and the past, 69–70; Said on, 56; Watt on, 55

Orientalism, 51, 53, 56

Pāṇini: on *āścarya*, 62; sūtras cited, 58–59 (P1.4.29), 60 (P4.2.60), 106n20 (P6.1.147)
Patañjali: on *aitihāsikaḥ*, 60; and narration, 58–59
pathos, 48; and exclusion, 73–74; Frye on, 73–74; of historicality, 72–74; Wordsworth as master of, 73
Phenomenology of Spirit (Hegel), 17, 20
poetry: age of, 7, 16, 17; Condillac on, 13; Indian, Hegel on, 9, 38; and pathos, 73; and philosophy, 86; priority of, 12; privilege of, 23; distinguished from prose, 7, 12–13; and *rasa*, 63; Vico on, 13
Prehistory, 4, 23, 24, 37, 44, 54; and colonialism, 44–45; outside the limit, 48; distinguished from World-history, 23, 35, 40, 43
prose: in Bangla, 11–12; as a condition of being, 16, 18, 22, 46, 73; Condillac on, 13–14; Derrida on, 13; and everyday, 19, 20; Hegel on, 15, 16, 18, 24; of history, 15, 16, 24–47 passim, 54, 70, 72, 73; of life, 20, 46; distinguished from poetry, 7, 12, 14–15; of the world, 7–23 passim, 24, 45, 46, 72

Rabindranath Tagore: on his childhood experiences, 77–79, 87, 96–97; on creativity, 82, 87, 89–90, 96–99 passim; and his critique of historiography, 6, 72, 75–99 passim; debate with younger writers, 76, 95; on the historicality of everyday, 91–94, 98–99; and the limit of World-history, 5–6; on literature and historiography, 89–90, 95–99; on

narrative and event, 89; on his poetic development, 77–79; on seeing, 77, 80–81, 95–99 passim; on the Upanisads, 85–86
Rāma, 66, 67
The Rāmāyaṇa, 105n6, 110; Hegel on, 38; as *itihāsa*, 51, 52; as a narrative of wonder, 67–68; *rasa* in, 66
Ramkamal Sen, 52
Ramram Basu, 7, 15–16, 50; and Carey, 10–12, 52, 72; and modernity of his work, 11; *Raja Pratapaditya Caritra*, 11, 102n6; and World-history, 15–16
rasa, 48, 110; Abhinavagupta on, 66–67; as attunement, 63; defined, 63; distinguished from experience, 66; as self-knowledge, 67; Sushil Kumar De on, 63

Said, Edward: on beginning, 56; on cultural specificity of the novel, 56
Sāṃkhya, 110; concept of self in, 84
Sañjaya, 58, 60
Śaṅkara, 86, 107n7, 110; on *adhyāsa*, 31; and authority of his commentaries, 84–85
Sankha Ghosh, 76
Sanskrit, 27, 53, 109, 110, 111; drama, 27; *itihāsa* in, 50, 110; poetics, 62
Śaunaka, 57, 58
Sisir Kumar Das, 11
Sītā, 66
Spirit, 29, 32–35 passim; actualization of, 17, 25, 26, 27, 33, 34, 39; and freedom, 25, 30, 31, 32; and history, 14, 16, 17, 26; and nature, 25, 35; and self-consciousness, 17–18, 20, 24–25, 32, 35, 36; and stages of its progress, 16, 24, 26–27; and time, 14, 17, 27, 34; *see also* World-history
state, 24, 36; and *Aufhebung*, 3, 4; and civil society, 3, 72, 92; Hegel on, 9, 10, 15, 25, 36, 38, 39–46, 54, 71, 104n43; and history, 7, 9, 10, 15, 16, 36, 46, 47, 75; nation-state, 8, 48; as time's adversary, 71–72; and writing, 9, 10; *see also* statism
statism: and the colonial past, 5; Hegel's, 39–40, 44; and historiography, 5, 40, 45, 71–73; Tagore on, 90, 92
storyteller, 57, 58, 68; Bakhtin on, 69; grammarians' view of, 59; Herodotus and Thucydides as, 55; initiative of, 56; repetition urged on, 61; set apart from the story, 60
Surendranath Dasgupta, on the Upaniṣads, 82, 110
Sushil Kumar De, 11; on *rasa* theory, 63

Tagore. *See* Rabindranath Tagore
Taylor, Charles: on God and state in Hegel's philosophy, 104n43; on Hegel's notion of *Geist*, 28
temporality, 20, 21, 48, 92
Thucydides, and experience, 55, 71
time, 12, 14, 27, 29, 32–36 passim, 69, 70, 71, 79; being in, 46; as Chronos, 70; as everyday, 92; negativity of, 70–71; and story, 69; universal, 12; *see also* Spirit; state
translation, 76; of *itihāsa* into history, 48, 51, 52; of *rasa*, 63

Ugraśravā, 57, 58, 60
The Upaniṣads: Surendranath Dasgupta on, 82; Tagore's interpretation of, 82, 85–87

Vaiśampāyana, 58
Vedānta, 110; on *adhyāsa*, 31; concept of self in, 84–85; doctrine of illusion in, 110
Vico, Giambattista, 7; on language, 13, 14
Vyāsa, 58, 60, 61

Watt, Ian, on experience and the novel, 55
White, Hayden: on the premodern annal and chronicle, 102n10; on primitive elements of historical narrative, 50
Wittgenstein, Ludwig, and concept of the limit, 8, 16
wonder, 48–74 passim; as attunement, 63, 65, 66; Benjamin on, 65–66; differentiated from curiosity, 65; and experience, 66, 72; Greenblatt on, 64; Heidegger on, 65, 66; and historicality, 68; and listeners' expectation, 61–62; narratives of, 48, 62, 68; *rasa* of, 48, 63, 67; and repetition, 67–68; and *thaumazein*, 65, 66; in Western literature, 64
Wordsworth, William, 73
World-history, 3, 4, 34, 47, 48, 52, 73; concept of, 2; containment in, 6; eligibility for, 24, 35, 40–41; exclusion from, 10, 15, 16, 24, 35, 37, 38, 40–41, 50; as God's plan, 4, 28–29, 46; Hegel on, 2, 3, 4, 17, 23–33 passim; limit of, 4, 6, 7, 16, 48; morality of, 3, 4, 5, 43; and its narratives, 47, 49, 53, 71, 92; and Prehistory, 40, 43, 44, 45; Spirit and, 24–29 passim, 33, 34; stages of, 27, 32—34; and world-historical deeds, 4; and world-historical individuals, 4, 41

Yājñavalkya, 82, 107n7; to Maitreyī, 83–84